What Others Say About the Impact of this Book

"I have read your *No B.S. Time Management for Entrepreneurs* three times since mid-June. Here are the recommendations from your book I've implemented: I've set up a time-blocked schedule for myself; I keep phone time to a minimum, clustered; I link daily work to goals; I've re-arranged certain things, like my weekly commute to a research center, to off-peak times. My income for July topped $20,000.00—not the $10,000.00 I had as my goal. I know that for many of your folks this is merely a sneeze. But for me, it's a gigantic leap. And unheard of for a one-person genealogy business. Thank you seems like such a small acknowledgment for such a gigantic boost in my business productivity."

—Arlene H. Eakle, The Genealogical Institute, Utah

"People often ask me—'Tony, you're a writer, salesman, work-shop trainer, leader of multiple organizations, father of the three young children, in good physical shape. How do you pull it all off?' My answer: your book! I read it again every six months. The amazing thing is, I spend fewer hours, my income keeps rising. Your advice can make anyone a master of time, not a slave to it."

—Tony Rubleski, author of *Mind Capture*; V.P. Sales,
Captive Audience Advertising, Michigan

"After many years in the mortgage business, operating like the others, on call 24-7, I totally changed the way I do business, the access clients have to me, following the advice you gave me, that you've put in this book. Not only did it make my business more enjoyable, and gave me my life back, it has multiplied my income, and led to much better-behaved clients treating me with much more respect.

—Tracy Tolleson, Irwin Mortgage Pinnacle Club Marketing for Mortgage Brokers,
www.tracytolleson.com, Arizona

"My name is Sam Beckford. I'm 33 years old. My wife Valerie and I started our first dance studio from scratch in 1995, with no money, no investors, no contacts in the teaching business, and debt. We built our business up to three studio locations with over 2800 students in just eight years. Each of our locations makes a profit of over $100,000.00 a year. We are able to run our studios at this level without being slaves to our business. In addition, we host a large seminar twice a year and provide on-going coaching to other studio owners. For most of the year we work from our home office, only go into the studios three to four hours a week, take great vacations, and things run smoothly without us being there. Dan Kennedy has been a great mentor and example to me, not just for his smart marketing, but also for the way in which he controls his time, business, and life."

—Sam Beckford, Vancouver, B.C., Canada

NB.S.
TIME MANAGEMENT
FOR ENTREPRENEURS

THE ULTIMATE
NO HOLDS BARRED
KICK BUTT
TAKE NO PRISONERS
GUIDE TO TIME
PRODUCTIVITY
& SANITY

Dan Kennedy

EP
Entrepreneur.
Press

Editorial Director: Jere L. Calmes
Cover Design: David Shaw
Production and Composition: Eliot House Productions

This publication is designed to provide accurate and authoritative information in regard to the subject matter covered. It is sold with the understand-
ing that the publisher is not engaged in rendering legal, accounting or
other professional services. If legal advice or other expert assistance is
required, the services of a competent professional person should be sought.

Library of Congress Cataloging-in-Publication Data
  Kennedy, Dan S., 1954–
    No B.S. time management for entrepreneurs, no holds barred, kick butt,
  take no prisoners, guide to time productivity and sanity/by Dan Kennedy
      p.   cm.
    ISBN 1-932156-85-2
    1. Time managment. I. Title: Time management book. II. Title.
  HD69.T54K466 2004
  650.1'1—dc22   2004045553

Printed in Canada

09 08 07   10 9 8 7

Contents

Preface

It gets late early out here.

—YOGI BERRA

Wimps and Willie Lomans—beware! This book is not for the faint of heart, fawningly polite, or desperate to be liked.

Hopefully, you have picked up this book because you are an entrepreneur, your time is incredibly valuable to you, and you are constantly "running out of it."

If you know me, then you've also been motivated to get this book to find out how I manage to do all that I do. I have been asked so often, by, what seems like everybody who becomes familiar with my life, how the devil I fit it all in, that I sat down and wrote out the answer—this book. If you don't know me, then your curiosity about my methods may be further piqued by the description of my activities that follow this Preface. If you know me, skip that section.

As a very busy, sometimes frantic, time-pressured entrepreneur, awash in opportunity, too often surrounded by nitwits and slower-than-molasses-pouring-uphill folk, I understand your needs, desires, and frustrations. The multiple demands on an entrepreneur's time are *extraordinary*. So I am here to tell you that you need to take extraordinary measures to match those demands. Measures so radical and extreme that others may question your sanity. This is no ordinary time management book for the deskbound or the person doing just one job. This book is expressly for the wearer of many hats, the inventive, opportunistic entrepreneur who can't resist piling more and more responsibility onto his own shoulders, who has many more great ideas than time and resources to take advantage of them, who runs (not walks) through each day. I'm you, and this is our book.

As you have undoubtedly discovered, time is the most precious asset any entrepreneur possesses. Time to solve problems. Time to invent, create, think, and plan. Time to gather and assimilate information. Time to develop sales, marketing, management, and profit breakthroughs. Time to network. Probably not a day goes by that you don't shove something aside, sigh, and say to yourself: *"If I could only find an extra hour to work on this, it'd make a huge difference in our business."* Well, I'm going to give you that extra hour. But what we're about to do here together is much bigger than just eking out an extra hour here or there. We are going to drastically re-engineer your entire relationship with time.

I've had more than 25 plus years of high-pressure, high-wire-without-a-net entrepreneurial activity—starting, buying, developing, selling, succeeding in and failing in businesses, going broke, getting profoundly rich, and helping clients in hundreds of different fields. Here's what I've come to believe to be the single biggest "secret" of extraordinary personal, financial, and entrepreneurial success combined: the use or misuse (or abuse by others) of your time—the degree to which you achieve peak productivity—will determine your success. So this book is about everything that can be done to achieve peak personal productivity.

Just thinking about it is a big step in the right direction. Awareness helps a lot. There's a reason why you can't find a wall clock in a casino to save your life—those folks stealing your money do not want you to be aware of the passing of time. And that tells you something useful right there: you want to be very aware, all the time, of the passing of time. It is to your advantage to be very conscious of the passage and usage of minutes and hours. Put a good, big, easily visible, "nagging" clock in every work area. If you spend a lot of time on the phone, have and use a timer.

Beyond simple awareness, there are practical strategies, methods, procedures, and tools that the busiest, most pressured person can use to crowbar some breathing room into his schedule, to force others to cooperate with his exceptional needs, to squeeze just a bit more out of each day. In this book, I give you mine. You will undoubtedly be interested in some, disinterested in others, maybe even repulsed by a few. That's OK. Although it's generally a bad idea to hire an advice-giver and then choose only the advice you like, in this case, it IS a cafeteria, and you can pick and choose and still get value.

Now it is time to get to work.

—Dan S. Kennedy

Note: The original, first edition of the book was written and published in 1996. Yes, way back then! During that elapsed time of some eight years, 70,080 hours, 4,204,800 minutes, a lot has changed for me. I've ceased traveling like a maniac, dropping from an average 20 road-warrior days a month to four or five in some months, zero in many. To do this, I totally re-engineered my business and recently sold one of my businesses. In many respects, I have less responsibility, and by the time you read this, several hundred of my Inner Circle Members will have gathered to celebrate my official semi-retirement at age 49. Note the word "semi." (Glazer-Kennedy Inner Circle is a membership organization providing the author's *No B.S. Marketing Letter* and other services, with Silver, Gold, Gold+, Gold/VIP, and Platinum levels of membership. You will see references to a number of the Members throughout this book. Information is available at www.dankennedy.com.) Also since the publication of the first edition of this book, I have been diagnosed with diabetes; I lost 45 pounds and have kept it off for three years. To date, I have held the diabetes in check with nutrition, diet, exercise, and no prescription drugs. I've dramatically increased the time and energy given another endeavor of mine—harness racing. I own, at any given time, parts or all of 16 to 20 racehorses, and I drive in races most weeks. I am also, of course, eight years closer to the 19th hole. To paraphrase Yogi, it's getting later earlier.

How has all this changed the attitudes and beliefs I express about time in this book? Not much at all. If anything, the passing of time has evermore stiffened my resolve about safeguarding it, wisely investing it, enjoying it, and bringing wrath upon any who would steal it, waste it, or abuse it.

How has the passing of time changed my personal practices with regard to time? Only made them even more stringent, me more militant. I think I may have mellowed, gotten softer in other ways, but not when it comes to time. So this book accurately reflects my thoughts, my modus operandi today, is absolutely applicable today, and, I think, more critically important than when first conceived.

The big thing that has changed since this book's first publication is the large and growing number of my own clients, Inner Circle Members, and readers of prior editions who've adopted—many, timidly, even fearfully, and skeptically at first—the advice in this book and lived to be grateful for doing so. When I first wrote the book, I was more of a lone wolf but in this edition, I have added many stories, examples, experiences, and comments from others who benefited from my strategies.

I will welcome YOUR comments. You can fax me at 602-269-3113. No, you can't call me. Nor do I accept e-mail. You'll read why in this book.

For Those Unfamiliar with Dan Kennedy, a Brief Description of His Motivations for Militant Safeguarding and Control of His Time, and a Few of His Most Interesting Procedures

For more than 25 years, Dan Kennedy traveled extensively, often exceeding 120 to 130 travel days a year, presenting as many as 70 speaking engagements and seminars annually. In addition, he consulted with numerous clients, ran as many as four businesses simultaneously, and employed as many as 42 people and as few as one. He also wrote and had published at least one new book a year for eight consecutive years; wrote and saw published more than 100 other books, audiocassette programs, and home study courses; wrote and published two monthly newsletters the entire time; got involved in horseracing, and still took quite a few vacations every year.

Presently, he maintains a slightly saner schedule, notably with substantially reduced travel. Still, he has 63 clients in four different coaching/peer advisory groups, three of which meet for six days a year, and one for eight days a year. In one year, he also spends one day every month tele-coaching the same groups, works with 15 to 20 ongoing consulting clients and their projects simultaneously, writes direct-response ad and direct-mail copy for more than 50 clients, 200 projects a year, speaks at seminars ten times, has clients come to him for more than 30 consulting days, produces several TV infomercials, writes two monthly newsletters, writes at least one book, and drives in harness races two or more nights a week almost every week. And he takes vacations.

He has but one staffperson, in an office distant from his own home office. He takes no unscheduled incoming calls, does not own a cell phone, and stubbornly refuses to use e-mail. His office phones are answered "live" only one afternoon per week. He deals with the majority of his faxes and mail only once each week.

Entrepreneurs have traveled from England, Australia, New Zealand, Japan, Korea, Mexico, Argentina, Canada, and every nook and cranny of the United States and paid $2,000.00 to $5,000.00 each to attend his intensive, multi-day seminars on entrepreneurial success, in which the subject of time is always addressed. Kennedy is legendary within his Inner Circle Membership and clientele of thousands for his unusual modus operandi concerning time, and in this book, you get an inside look at the key strategies employed and the thinking of one of the most dedicated time and productivity managers to walk the earth!

It is significant that Kennedy is no longer alone in utilizing these methods—in fact, he has inspired countless business owners and sales professionals to make radical changes in the way they control their time, access, and people around them. A few of their comments appear at the beginning of this book.

"Nothing is worth more than this day. "
—Goethe

CHAPTER 1

How to Turn
Time into Money

*Eliminate the time between the idea and the act, and
your dreams will become realities.*

—DR. EDWARD L. KRAMER, INVENTOR OF THE SELF-IMPROVEMENT
SYSTEM KNOWN AS "SYNCHROMATICS"

What is "entrepreneurship" if not the conversion of your
knowledge, talent, guts, etc.— through investment of
your time—into money?

Starting with the very next chapter, we dive into very specific
how-to strategies, but first I think you'll find it useful to understand how I arrived at my philosophy of valuing time and how I
value time. I'll be the first to tell you: you can't eat philosophy,
but you do need your own philosophy of time valuing.

In time management books and in time management seminars, authors and speakers love to show off charts and graphs
depicting the dollar value of each workday hour, depending on
your income or the income you want to achieve. Maybe you've

sat through one of these little graph-and-pointer sessions before. You know, Mr. Lecturer up there, laptop computer wired into the overhead projector, lights dimmed, even a laser beam pointer in hand, so he can show off his beautiful five-color bar graph. If you use his numbers, for example, based on eight-hour workdays, presuming 220 workdays, earning $200,000.00 a year requires that each hour be worth $113.64.

And that looks great on the chart. And everybody in the room busily calculates what their hours have to be worth. Somebody who wants to make $100,000.00 a year figures $56 an hour—hey, I can do that. Plumbers, dentists, accountants, sales-people, most businesspeople say: cakewalk.

Unfortunately, it's all a pile of seminar room B.S.

Here's why: it's all based on eight-hour workdays. Eight hours a day. But there's not a soul on the planet who gets in eight *productive* hours a day. Not even close. You see, the workday hour is one thing, *the productive hour*—or what I call the billable hour— is another. Elsewhere in this book, there's a definition of productivity you may want to use to determine which of your hours are productive.

Now, if you happen to be an attorney, none of this matters. It seems lawyers bill out hours whether productive or not. Rodney King, famous for getting beat up by the Los Angeles police, had attorneys who billed for such things as escorting King to his birthday party and even thinking about his case while commuting. Here's a joke: 35-year-old lawyer in perfect health suddenly drops dead. He gets to Saint Peter at The Gate and argues: "You guys screwed up. You pulled me up here early." Saint Peter checks his clipboard and says, "No sir. Judging by your total billable hours, you're 113 years old and we're late." *Lawyers.*

But the rest of us can only collect on genuinely productive hours.

Can One "Number" Change Your Life?

So let's go back to the math game and assume that $200,000.00 is your *base earnings target*. (We'll talk more about what that term means later.) How many of your hours will be genuinely productive, directly generating revenue? How many will be otherwise consumed: commuting, filling out government paperwork, dealing with vendors, emptying the trash cans, whatever? Let's say it's one-third productive, two-thirds other. That's pretty generous, by the way. One study of Fortune 500 CEOs locked in at an average of 28 productive *minutes* a day. Lee Iacocca once told me he figured top CEOs might average 45 productive minutes per day—the rest of the day fighting off time-wasting B.S. like a frantic fellow futilely waving his arms at a swarm of angry bees on attack. But we'll say: one-third. Roughly, only one of three hours counts as "billable." So you've got to multiply the $113.64 times three, to get $340.92. This becomes your governing number for $200,000.00 a year.

My personal number is a bit higher, but if the $340.92 were MY governing number, as it was a couple years ago, here's how I would have to use it.

First, it'd be on my mind constantly. Is what I'm doing worth $340.92 an hour to do it?

Second, it puts a meter on others' consumption of your time—that unnecessary 12-minute phone conversation just cost $68.18. This exercise is extremely beneficial. This forces you to think in terms of "investment" and "expense." It helps you *quantify* what is going on in your life.

Third, for me it sets the base cost for hours given to a speaking engagement, consulting assignment, copywriting assignment, and other things I do that are directly billable. And if you do anything but earn a fixed salary, you have to weigh this base cost against every activity, to set your fee or to decide whether or not to bother.

When I wrote the first edition of this book in 1996, I was charging about $3,500.00 to write an advertisement or sales letter for a client. Today, it starts at $15,000.00 to $21,000.00, and runs as high as twice that, plus royalties. But let's say I still charged a client $3,500.00 to write an advertisement. The naive would say that I just made $3,500.00. After all, I didn't have any "hard" cost; I just sat in a room and thought, then just sat at a computer and wrote. But if you think that way, you'll never make big money. If it took me six hours to write that ad, there WAS a "hard" cost of $340.92 times 6, which equals $2,045.52. If it took me twice that long, I lost money.

If you travel in your business, you've really got to watch this. As I write this, I live in a couple of different places. If I'm in Phoenix, a business meeting in Los Angeles will take, at most, two days: one half day to travel, a day for the meeting, one half day back. Maybe even less. But if I'm in Cleveland, a meeting in Los Angeles will take three full days. One full day more. Using the $340.92 hour number, it costs $2,727.36 MORE to go to the meeting.

I've learned to think about this a lot. For example, as of this writing, my one-day, basic consulting fee is $8,300.00 (plus expenses) if I travel to the client but only $7,800.00 if the client comes to me. Why? Because it's worth money to me to stay home! I'm buying time. I've maintained this sort of fee differential for years, but beginning in 2002, I started simply refusing to go to clients and only offering available dates in the cities where I live.

Many of my clients and Inner Circle Members have adopted some variation of differential pricing in their businesses. An attorney, Mace Yampolsky, charges a higher fee to personally handle your case, a lower fee to supervise the handling of your case by his staff attorneys, and yet a lower fee to only consult with your attorney regarding your case. Dr. Charles Martin charges different fees if he personally performs the dentistry rather than if you use other dentists also providing Martin Method Dentistry.

Many years ago, when I was in the field, selling, I quickly figured out that you could fit in two, three, four, or five appointments per day, depending on how you routed yourself. A salesman half as good at selling as a competitor but twice as good at efficiently routing himself and clustering prospects makes the same amount of money. Today, when I get on an airplane, I have "clustered" as much productive activity as possible into that one trip. We'll talk about this in greater detail in Chapter 8.

By working at home, as a writer, consultant, and tele-coach, as opposed to going to an office, I make a lot of money each day just by not commuting. I have conditioned myself to go directly from bed to shower to work in 15 minutes. If I were leaving the house to go to an office, I'd have those 15 minutes plus another half hour, maybe an hour commute, than another 15 minutes getting settled in at the office. Not to mention the commute at end of day.

In whatever ways you can, in your business, you need to seek leverage. In terms of work productivity, leverage is, in essence, the difference between the base cost for your hour and the amount of money you get for it or from it. One good way to evaluate your personal effectiveness is measuring and monitoring this differential, hour by hour, for a week.

Now, let's go back to the term: *base earning target*. Since you are your own boss, you write your own paycheck, and you decide how much that paycheck is going to be. For most entrepreneurs, that number is—whatever's left! This is a huge mistake, for two reasons: it indicates zero planning, and it means you pay yourself last, the number one reason entrepreneurs wind up broke. So, let's reverse all that, and start with the planning. You've got to decide how much money you're going to take out of your business or businesses this year, in salary, perks, contributions to retirement plans, and so on. What is that number?

I'll tell you this: eight out of ten entrepreneurs I ask cannot come up with this number.

Anyway, if you do not have a base income target, then you cannot calculate what your time must be worth, which means you cannot make good decisions about the investment of your time, which means you are not exercising any real control over your business or life at all. You are a wandering generality. Is that what you want to do—*just wander around and settle for whatever you get?*

Now, you may not have a situation that lends itself to clear-cut billable hours as I do, so how can this strategy work for you? It has to. It's even more important to you than to me. Let's say you own six stores. Each store has a manager. Hey, this is complicated. Well, you'll have to decide how much of the business' bottom line profit goal will be provided by the managers whether you sleep or work and how much is still inextricably linked to you. If you want $500,000.00 at the

> *E*ntrepreneurs should think about the purpose of business. A lot of business owners lose sight of that altogether. The purpose of a business is to make its owner rich. The first responsibility of the owner is to extract money from the business, not leave it locked up in it or, worse, put money into it.

bottom line, and you figure half is dependent on you, you've got a $250,000.00 target.

For me, it's reasonably precise. For you, it may not be such an exact science. But that's OK. I promise you that coming up with a number, even if it is arrived at through some pretty questionable calculations, is still a whole lot better than not having a number at all. Having a number is going to make such a dramatic change in so many of the decisions you make, habits you cultivate, and people you associate with, that the benefits will be so extraordinary, it won't matter if the original method of getting to a number had a technical flaw or two buried in it. At least for the sake of our conversation, in this book, get a number: YOUR base earnings target for the next full calendar year. (See Figure 1.1.) Divide it by the number of workday hours. Multiply it to allow for unproductive vs. productive hours. If you haven't a better estimate of that, use

FIGURE 1.1: Calculating Your Base Earnings Target

Base Earnings Target:	$ 500,000
Divided by (220 days x 8 = 1,760) work hours in a year	÷ 1,760
= base hourly Number	$ 289.68
Times productivity vs. nonproductivity multiple	X 3
= What your time must be worth per hour:	$ 846.04

the three time multiple I've used here. Now you have what your time is supposed to be worth per hour. Divided by 60, per minute.

That little number may just change your life.

It's sort of like a heart attack—or, in my own case, a diabetes diagnosis—being required to really get somebody to change their eating and exercise habits.

A lot of your decision-making gets easy with this number staring you in the face. It's hard to con yourself with this number staring you in the face. In fact, I suggest having it stare you in the face a lot until you internalize it. Write your number "$*846.* ⁷⁷ Per Hour" on a bunch of colorful 4 x 6-inch cards, in bold black letters, and stick those cards up in places where you work and will see them often.

Generally speaking, two business life changes probably come to mind immediately, with this number staring you in the face:

First, you realize that you've got to surround yourself with people who understand and respect the value of your time and behave accordingly. This is not easy. And they will forget, over time. Familiarity breeds contempt. Periodically, you will have to re-orient them. You also must get people who do not respect the value of your time out of your business life. If you let people who

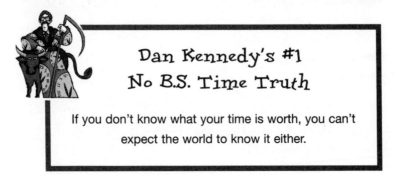

Dan Kennedy's #1 No B.S. Time Truth

If you don't know what your time is worth, you can't expect the world to know it either.

do not understand and respect the value of your time hang around, you won't even have a fighting chance.

Second, you have to eliminate the need for doing or delegate those tasks and activities that just cannot and do not match up with the mandated value of your time.

How Low Can You Go in Valuing Time?

I grew up in Ohio, where people spend their weekends shoveling snow in the winter, cutting grass in the spring and summer, and raking leaves in the fall. Used to make me crazy to drive around and see somebody in my sales organization out shoveling, mowing, or raking. I'd say: if your time isn't worth more than the $5 an hour you could give some neighborhood kid to do this, you should be shot. Plus, you're robbing some kid out of the money. When I moved to Arizona, I envisioned sand, rocks, and cactus; nothing to shovel or mow. Guess what? A bunch of folks bring grass with 'em and stick it everywhere, then alternate between watering it and mowing it. Others, with "desert landscaping" can be found out there raking their gravel—like cats in litter boxes! What conclusion did I draw from all that? Most people will find ways to avoid confrontive productivity and will waste their time, even if they have to work at it!

Well, my "philosophy of time valuing" can be boiled down to this: every one of my working hours has to be worth a certain amount of money; I do everything I can to create and protect that value; and anybody screwing that up had better watch out.

Another, related issue is "project valuing" or "opportunity valuing" or "account valuing" for salespeople. In short, a "thing" has to be worth X-dollars, whatever you decide X must be, for you to even touch it, think about it, or be involved with it. Many of my best clients have adopted this idea and now have their own litmus test, helpful in quickly and decisively saying yea or nay to whatever comes along.

For example, my Platinum Member Matt Furey started in business only a handful of years ago with a $10,000.00 minimum: a new product he might develop or a new marketing campaign he might initiate had to be worth at least $10,000.00 to him or he'd pass. Today his number is $100,000.00. He has mastered the wisdom that just because something is a viable opportunity doesn't mean it's an opportunity for you, just because something is doable doesn't mean you should do it.

Most sales professionals hang onto clients and accounts that consume far, far more time than they can ever be worth. Better to send them to a competitor. Most entrepreneurs perpetuate projects that consume far, far more time—theirs or employees'—than they're worth. I've done it more times than I care to confess. But I'm getting much better at NOT doing it with each passing year. As a good reminder, my friend Lee Milteer, a top business performance coach, and the host/interviewer on my Renegade Millionaire System audio program (for information about my Renegade Millionaire System and once-a-year seminar go to www.renegademillionaire.com), gave me a wall plaque as my 49th birthday gift that reads:

Dan's Other Business

It Seemed Like a Good Idea
At The Time, Inc.

CHAPTER 2

How to Drive a Stake
Through the Hearts of the Time Vampires Out to Suck You Dry

And even as they looked the thing tore the throat out of Hugo Baskerville, on which, as it turned its blazing eyes and ripping jaws upon them, the three shrieked with fear and rode for dear life, still screaming, across the moor.

—FROM *THE HOUND OF THE BASKERVILLES* BY SIR ARTHUR CONAN DOYLE

Time Vampires are needy, thirsty, selfish, vicious creatures who, given an opportunity, will suck up all of your time and energy, leaving you white, weak, and debilitated. Once they have found a good meal, they start coming back every day—so, even though you regenerate yourself with a meal, a night's sleep, and a vial of vitamins, it's to no avail; they will be waiting for you tomorrow just where they left you yesterday, eager to once again suck every ounce of life from your veins. Being able to recognize these vampires on sight is the first step in protecting yourself from them. Being willing to deal with them as you would a vile, evil, blood-sucking creature of the dark is the first step in freeing yourself from them.

Maybe the most insidious of all the Time Vampires is Mr. Have-You-Got-a-Minute? He lurks in the shadows in the hall outside your office, near the elevator, near the cafeteria, in the bushes next to the parking lot, wherever it is possible to catch you off guard. If you give in to him a few times, he becomes emboldened and starts "dropping in" to your office or home. He disarms you with "Have you got a minute?" or "I just need a couple minutes of your time" or "I just have one quick question." He has a unique knack of pulling this stunt right when you are in the middle of doing something incredibly important—getting mentally prepared for a most important phone call, or at some similar moment. If you are in his vicinity all day, he'll also "drop by" a dozen times a day—each time needing "just a minute."

Each time he drops by, picture him sinking his teeth into your neck and sucking out a pint or two. That IS the effect he has.

The temptation to give in to this particular vampire is almost irresistible. First of all, it just seems easier to deal with his "one quick question" immediately than to put him off and have it hanging over you for later. Second, it *feels* rude and unreasonable to refuse him. But the truth is, he deserves no courtesy whatsoever. He is telling you that your time is less valuable than his, that whatever you are doing is unimportant and easily interrupted. He is, in street jargon, dissing you to the max. So, go ahead and stick a stake through his heart without a moment's remorse.

Here's the stake.

I'm busy right now.
Let's meet at 4:00 P.M. for 15 minutes,
and tackle everything on your list at one time.

This stops this bloodthirsty vampire in his tracks. Freezes him, like a deer in headlights. Next, it "teaches" this vampire a new discipline. Of course, he won't get it the first time. Or the second. He'll keep trying for a while. But if you whip out this same stake every time, over and over again, and jam it firmly through his chest, eventually he *will* get the message. Someday, he'll call you and say something like: "I have five things I need to go over with you. When can we get together?" After you pick yourself up off the floor, you can congratulate yourself on having defanged and housebroken a vampire.

"They're in a Meeting"

The next most dangerous Time Vampire is *Mr. Meeting*. Some people seem to do nothing but attend meetings. Just as I was finishing this book, a client of mine dragged me into a 20-minute, four-person conference call to discuss when we could have the next, longer conference call to plan a meeting. Geez.

Being in meetings is *seductive*. It is a way to feel important. It's also a great way to hide from making and taking responsibility for decisions. *Meetingitis* is a disease that turns businesses into unproductive, indecisive, slow-moving coffee klatches. (The two toughest CEO's I know hold only "stand-up meetings." No chairs.)

According to a study published in *Corporate Meetings Magazine* in the late 1990s when I wrote the first edition of this book, people were spending an average of 20 to 40 hours per month in meetings, an increase over previous years. The average time spent in meetings by managers was 1.7 hours per day, and executives spent 50% of their time in meetings. Those surveyed said that the most productive meetings lasted under an hour, but most meetings lasted two hours or longer. It is my observation that this situation has only worsened, year after year. Even

The other day, I called a company, pressed for some information, and got this from the frazzled receptionist: "Everybody's in meetings. I don't know anything. Please call back some other time when there might be somebody who knows something available."

though we've all been offered, and most have accepted, a whole new arsenal of gadgets and technologies supposed to make communication more efficient, everybody I try to connect with is *in a meeting*.

You need to stop and ask yourself: do I really need to be in—or hold—this meeting? Is there a more time-efficient way to handle this? A conference call? A memo circulated to each person? Heck, a posting on a bulletin board. Or an Internet site. An e-mail. Hey, anything BUT another meeting.

If you are going to hold a meeting, there are several stakes you can use to stop the vampires from making it an endless "blood klatch." (Time Vampires love meetings, because a bunch of blood-rich victims gather in one place at one time. It's like a buffet.)

1. Set the meeting for immediately before lunch or at the end of the day, so the vampires are eager to get it done and over with, turn into bats, and fly out of there.
2. Don't serve refreshments.
3. Circulate a written agenda in advance.
4. Have and communicate a clear, achievable objective for the meeting.

This refreshment thing's a big tip, by the way. My friend Dave Petito, a great TV infomercial producer, and I both used to get paid to attend meetings for the same company. These took place at the firm's palatial Beverly Hills office or sometimes its CEO's home. Either place, the table was laden end to end with a fabulous array of food. Bagels, five flavors of cream cheese, salmon, imported cheeses, sandwich meats, croissants, muffins, cookies. Really good grub. Added at least an hour or more to every meeting—after all, you can't advise with your mouthful. This company has long since gone out of business. I wonder why.

If you must *attend* a meeting, you also have some stakes available so you can slay Mr. Meeting.

1. Determine in advance what information you are to contribute, then do it with a prepared, minimum-time, maximum-impact presentation.

2. Have an exit strategy: someone coming in to get you at a certain time, a pre-arranged call on your cell phone, whatever. You can then excuse yourself only long enough to make a call and return if you need to—but you probably won't.

Playing Trivial Pursuit

Another Time Vampire to watch out for is *Mr. Trivia*. He either can't or doesn't want to differentiate between the important and unimportant, minor and major.

This vampire's talent is getting others off track, getting you to set aside your carefully organized list of priorities in favor of his—and, more often than not, his agenda will be of minimal importance. Mr. Trivia will interrupt to tell you just about anything, ranging from the building being on fire to the office supply store having delivered blue pens instead of black pens. Usually it'll be the latter.

The best way to deal with this one is to drop a big silver cross around his neck and kick him off the parapet of your castle. But failing the opportunity of doing that, you need another stake—this one is to interrupt the interrupter:

> I have an exceptionally busy day, so I am only dealing with 9s and 10s on a 1-10 scale. Everything else MUST wait until tomorrow.
>
> Are you convinced that what you want to talk to me about is a 9 or 10?

He will say, "No, but—" and then you must again rudely interrupt him: "No buts. Thanks. We'll get to it tomorrow." Then physically get away. (If he's in YOUR office, you leave.)

He will be offended. Good. The odds of him holding the trivial matter over until tomorrow and bringing it back to you are less than 50–50. He'll go sink his teeth into somebody else's throat. Or maybe even resolve it on his own. But he *won't* patiently wait until tomorrow.

Oh Boy, It's Soap Opera Time!

Have you ever watched soap opera diva Susan Lucci overact? Someone can walk into a room and say, "Ronald has just been murdered and is lying outside on the lawn with a giant metal pink flamingo stuck through his chest," or walk in and say, "It's raining outside," and get the same massive reaction: crying, sobbing, pulling hair, chest heaving, body twisting, overacting. Well, some people are just like Susan in real life. They turn everything into an emotional crisis. They react to everything emotionally. They magnify everything's importance. And if you're not careful, they'll pull you right into the drama. When they do, visualize them sticking in the IV and taking out a quart.

The other problem with these particular vampires is that, at the very least, they make you give up your time to attempt to put them back together emotionally. They guilt you into giving them your shoulder to cry on. And while they're resting their head on your shoulder, they're sticking their teeth into your neck.

Some people have the amazing ability to turn every molehill into a mountain. If you happen to have some of these overreactive, emotionally wrought weepers in your organization, get rid of them if you can. If you can't do that, then, personally, stay away from them. There are two ways to drive them away.

1. Cut to the core of their problem (which is usually glaringly obvious) and tell them what to do. This is not what they want. They don't want solutions; they want soap opera. Spoil their fun and they'll go looking for blood elsewhere.
2. Take over the conversation by launching into a long, boring, pointless story; say: "That reminds me of a time when my Uncle Harold was in the dust bowl during the great Depression. This story will help you. Here goes!" In other words, turn into a vampire yourself and start sucking.

Are There Other Time Vampires?

There are almost as many different varieties of Time Vampires as there are birds or butterflies. Your productivity multiplies as you get better and better skilled at spotting them and driving stakes through their hearts.

Ask yourself if you're doing something now to invite the time vampires in for a feast. If so, stop doing it.

How I Stupidly Put Out the Welcome Mat for the Time Vampires and Let Them Suck Me Dry

In an article I read in some business magazine, a story was told of how a brave CEO, in one of his first acts as president of a medical center, yanked his office door from its hinges and suspended it from the lobby ceiling to demonstrate his commitment to an open-door policy. This was applauded by the magazine as some giant act of courage and creativity. I chuckled when I read this. This guy has my sympathy. To the management theorists who get all wet and excited when they hear this sort of thing, I say: c'mon out into the real world, where they eat their young every day, and try this yourself. You won't last a week.

This tactic is nothing new or revolutionary or innovative. Heck, I made that same mistake about 20 years ago.

Right after I took the helm of a barely afloat manufacturing company, I pried the office door off the hinges, nailed it to the wall sideways, and proclaimed that, from now on, the president's office had a true "open-door policy." High drama. Incredible stupidity.

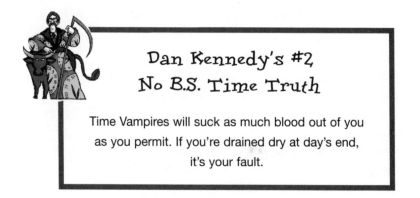

Dan Kennedy's #2 No B.S. Time Truth

Time Vampires will suck as much blood out of you as you permit. If you're drained dry at day's end, it's your fault.

All day long, an endless parade of Time Vampires. Suck, suck, suck. By the end of the day, my neck looked like a pincushion. I was whiter than typing paper. Almost transparent. Slumped over my desk, not even enough energy left to sit upright. Eyes glazed over. Breathing shallow. I'm telling you, they just lined up, marched in, and happily took turns siphoning me dry. The only thing that stopped them from slicing me up like London Broil and consuming me completely was the clock reaching 5:00 P.M. I put out the vampire welcome mat, and they took me up on the invitation. My fault, of course.

This sort of thing looks just great on paper. Unfortunately, a lot of ideas—like this one—is put on paper by goofball authors (!) who haven't a lick of real-world experience, have their butts safely parked on a bucolic college campus somewhere, and have a ball dreaming up clever-sounding psychobabble buzzwords and hot, new management theories to baffle and bedazzle us with. Well, don't believe everything you read.

CHAPTER 3

Stopping "Productivus Interruptus" Once and for All

My life is one long obstacle course, with me being the chief obstacle.

—JACK PAAR

I nterruptions destroy many office- or desk-bound individuals' productivity.

Put a stop to interruptions: multiply your productivity. It is that simple.

After reading a study claiming that the average business owner is interrupted once every eight minutes, I had three of my clients who spend all day on their business premises put a watch on it for a day. One reported a better average: once per ten. The other two, six, and the third hollered, "Hey, I need a stopwatch."

When I used to go to my offices in a place where I was under the same roof with my staff, I found that to be about par—*if I let it happen.* And, as a big thumb rule, the more employees or associates you've got, the more you get interrupted. Some years back, I suddenly wound up with a staff of 42 people thrust upon me. For a while, I was interrupted every eight *seconds,* not every eight minutes. It was embarrassing to ultimately realize that this was all my fault. I permitted, even invited the interruptions. And I learned to stop them.

There are many reasons for these interruptions, and almost none of them have to do with necessity! If you're going to achieve peak personal productivity in such an environment, here are the five self-defense, time-defense tactics you'll have to use:

1. Get lost
2. Don't answer the phone
3. Fix the fax
4. Set the timer on the bomb
5. Be busy and be obvious about it

Get Lost

Your first tactic—simple inaccessibility. When I was in the office I got asked lots of questions that I knew the people figured out for themselves when I wasn't there, so my being there, and being accessible, actually diminished *their* productivity as well as mine. The answer is not to be there at all. Some entrepreneurs think they have to set a leadership example by being the first person there, to turn on the lights, and the last person to leave, to turn off the lights. I made this mistake, and it IS a huge mistake. Leadership is *not* about outworking everybody.

I learned by traveling that my people functioned just as well or better with me as an absentee leader as they did with me onsite. When I was on the road and inaccessible, they handled 80% of everything on their own, most of it satisfactorily, some with excellence, and a little bit unsatisfactorily but almost always repairable. And they asked me about the other 20% quickly and efficiently, in brief phone conversations or via fax. Since that worked okay when it had to, there's no reason it couldn't work all the time. So, I stopped going in to the office, period. I had a fax at home and at the office, so when I was in town, I stayed at home and worked there largely interrupted. When necessary, I faxed or phoned in; they phoned or faxed me.

Today, I live and work at my Ohio home more than anywhere else. I have only one staff person, and she is in the office—in Phoenix. About as far from underfoot as can be. Almost without exception, we talk by phone once a day, usually for less than 20 minutes; I get truly urgent faxes once a day; and once a week I get a nicely organized box of other faxes, mail, and a list of questions. She is far better organized in dealing with me than she'd be were I there or more accessible. I am far better organized in dealing with her. I'm certain it equates to at least two hours of productivity saved per day for both of us, and in my world, that's a whole pile of money. A lot more than the weekly FedEx bill.

Dozens of my clients have mimicked these practices, with very good result. In fact, I can name more than 30—some running small businesses like mine with only one or two staff, others running businesses doing as much as $30 million a year—who have offices they seldom visit—from no more than once a week to as seldom as once a month. Chet Rowland, who owns one of the largest and most profitable pest control companies in Florida, as well as a marketing, training and coaching company serving the entire pest control industry, has sales, administrative, technical, and in-the-field, on-the-truck employees. He goes to the office no more than twice a month. His right-hand person comes to his home for a meeting once a week. He gets daily statistics and information electronically. He works in a home office at his sprawling lakeside home or at his beachfront condo. He travels often with no anxiety about being away from the office, because he's always away from the office. He gets so much more accomplished than he would if in that office eight hours a day, it can't even be measured.

I have a friend, a CEO of a $4 or $5 million-a-year business, who can't work at home; he has six kids, two dogs, one spouse. So he has a small $200-a-month office in town, about halfway between his home and his manufacturing facility. It has no phone and no fax. And he spends most of his time there.

He and I agree:

Dan Kennedy's #3
No B.S. Time Truth

If they can't find you, they can't interrupt you.

Another business owner I know has been weaning his staff from him and weaning himself from being in his office every minute, poking his nose in everything, second-guessing everybody. To his shock and surprise, things have been going well. A few people in his organization have risen to the occasion. A few have proven unable to adjust and been fired. Overall, sales and profits are up. He is finding time to invent and work on "special projects" he's been thinking about for years. And for the first time ever, he's taking an entire month of vacation, at a rented beach cottage, several states away from his business. For the first time in 30 years, he's really becoming a business owner instead of being owned by a business.

If you *are* going to be in your office with the rest of your staff, then, contrary to my dumb open door management experiment, it is very important that you have a CLOSED DOOR POLICY. You need some times when everybody knows—because of the closed door, red light, stuffed purple dragon in the hallway, whatever—that you are 100% uninterruptible. And if you want to sit in there and take a nap, you go right ahead. It's none of their damned business.

Don't Answer the Phone

Next, you've got to get control over the telephone. I think the phone is Peak Productivity Enemy Number One, and your people will be in cahoots with it until you break them of the habit. People somehow get conditioned that they must respond to the phone when it rings, and believe you should too. At home, on their own time, people will run dripping from the bathtub, jump up from the dinner table, even "coitus interruptus" to answer the phone. It's incredible how cowed by Mr. Bell's invention most people are. Ring. Run. Respond. *Nuts.*

So, first, let me offer a bit of philosophy: you have absolutely no legal, moral, or other responsibility to answer the phone or take a call unless you want to. At home, I routinely take the phone off the hook to take a shower, eat a meal, take a nap, watch a favorite TV program or, well, for other things too. There's nothing—and I mean nothing—happening on earth that can't or won't wait an hour. Or two. You should carry that attitude into your work too. Different people need different levels of control over telephone interruptions, but I do not believe anybody ought to be wide open to in-bound calls. This is like walking around with a "Kick Me" sign tacked to your back. If you take inbound calls as they come, you are constantly stopping work on a task of known priority in favor of something or someone of unknown priority. You are turning control of your day over to the unknown. And at the end of most days, you'll be worn out, but you won't have gotten to do most of the things you wanted to do.

Personally, I have very rarely encountered an inbound call damaged by a day's delay in response. Most of my important calls are forwarded to me while traveling, and I start trying to return them the next day. A lot of the calls wait three, four, even five days before I take time to return them. Guess what? Occasionally, somebody's aggravated—which is their problem, not mine—but I have yet to notice this approach costing me any money. Not a nickel. In fact, ironically, in my business (and in many), being somewhat difficult to get to actually helps rather than hinders securing new clients and having those clients appreciate and respect your time and assistance. Rightly or wrongly, most folks don't put a lot of value on getting to the wise man at the *bottom* of the mountain. (I talk about this, in the context of "Takeaway Selling," in my book *No B.S. Sales Success.*)

The Take-with-You Phone

Now, the cell phone—an evil invention if there ever was one. People really feel compelled to answer these things 24/7. It is the ultimate interruption welcome mat, and it has amazing, mysterious powers over its owner.

As comedian Dennis Miller says, I don't want to get off on a rant here, but... increasingly, I am noticing men standing at urinals in public restrooms taking care of business while talking on the phone simultaneously. Look, if you can't even pee in peace, you are not Mr. Super-Important. You are Mr. Super-Stupid.

Personally, I refuse to own or use one at all. I had one for two weeks once. Wound down the car window one day and threw it as far as I could. Never been tempted again.

If you insist on carrying one of these miserable things, have the good sense to turn it off. A lot. Like to walk to lunch with coworkers or friends, eat, and actually digest what you eat. Or pee. Or, say, navigate your SUV down the side of a mountain, on an icy, curvy road. And have the common decency to turn it off and shut up when you are seated next to me on an airplane before I ram it down your throat.

In my seminars, by the way, we assess a $100.00 fine anytime a cell phone erupts. And confiscate the offending phone for the duration.

Often, the offenders have paid $2,000.00 to $5,000.00 to be in the room. Many are also very good clients. I don't care. I will not tolerate it. I warn everybody, I put some big, beefy bruiser in charge of collecting, and I take the money. If you can't have your life sufficiently in order to pay uninterrupted attention and be courteous to others, I'd prefer you stay home and annoy someone else. I think restaurants and theaters ought to collect them when you come in and give them back when you leave, like civilized saloons did with gunslingers' weapons.

The pay phone in a booth with a folding door on it was a wonderfully civilized thing.

And a word to business owners, salespeople, and my pathetically desperate and paranoid speaking colleagues who devoutly believe they must be instantly accessible at any and every moment to every client and prospective client to prevent that client from dialing the next number and doing business with whomever answers instantly: if you are that interchangeable, that mundane and ordinary a commodity, you've got big, big problems, far bigger than you can solve by answering your cell while you're on the can. Turn off the thing long enough to read my *No B.S. Sales Success* book. *That's* urgent.

Maybe this will help: picture the poor fellow walking around with cell phone in hand or on belt, or worse, with headphones on, is like a big, dumb dog with collar and leash. Tug, tug, tug. Yap, yap, yap. Pant, pant, pant.

If you walk upright, you ought to behave better than this. And resent the leash.

Your "Steel Curtain" Telephone Defense

If you buy into this tactic at all, you will obviously need a good screening system. What will protect you from the telephone? If you have a live person, a receptionist or secretary or a receptionist plus a secretary, that's probably best. (If not, you'll have to use voice mail or an answering machine.) Your receptionist or secretary needs a continually updated "VIP list" of people from whom you will almost always take an incoming call, regardless of what else you may be doing. This prevents you from missing calls you really want, and it allows your assistant to screen all the other calls with great confidence.

Keeping this VIP list up to date helps prevent screening faux pas, however, even when a faux pas occurs, you must never sacrifice your assistant to the cause. You must support the person doing your screening 100% of the time. A screener can only do the job if she has complete confidence in what she's doing.

If you want staff to consistently put up a "Steel Curtain Defense" comparable in strength and reliability to the famous Pittsburgh Steelers' steel curtain defense of their glory years, you have to give them the right tools, equipment, and support.

Ÿou might wonder who's on my VIP List. I'll appease your curiosity. At any one given time, there are a dozen or so key private clients on that list—people paying me sizable sums of money. I have several very close associates on the list. A few very close friends. And that's it. I'd say that a VIP list with more than two dozen people on it is not a VIP list at all. In my case, even the VIPs can't get through to me immediately, because I'm not there, but they will typically get a return call the same day or the next day. On a given day, a client might be given a direct line to where I'm working, under extreme circumstances, but for one-time use only. Oh, and even at the office, my staff person only answers "live" one afternoon a week, which is published and known to clients. Otherwise, they get my voice mail. I really do have a steel curtain defense.

You have to decide on the severity of the screening to be done. In my case, on any given day, I'll get a few VIP calls and up to two dozen calls from other people of unknown priority, including prospective new clients, book reviewers, media contacts, and salespeople. If I were in my office for the whole day and took these calls as they occurred, and each one averaged only three minutes, I would have let loose of an hour. But much more importantly, I would have been interrupted 24 times! The three minutes given each call would have cost me another ten minutes added, required to get back in gear after each interruption; 13 minutes times 24 calls equals FIVE HOURS of lost time.

However, because I travel and am rarely in my office, most of each day's non-VIP calls accumulate, so after a week, I may have as many as *120* calls to supposedly return. Considering all this, I have a very tough-minded policy. First, all callers are asked for their reason for calling. People refusing to provide good information about their reason for calling NEVER gets a return call; in fact, they never even get entered on my call log. My staff person is asked to throw them into the trash; this eliminates a lot of junk.

Second, prospective clients are asked to send information in writing, by mail or fax, so that I can look at it at my convenience and have the flexibility of responding as I judge best: calling, writing, sending information before calling, delegating, or referring elsewhere. If they won't do that, they NEVER get to me. Salespeople are told pretty much the same thing. If they won't play by my rules, they NEVER get through. The "tone' is polite but firm. I tend to return calls only once or twice a week, more often than not via pre-arranged, back-to-back, time-limited phone appointments.

I know, you're mumbling about the 52 reasons *you* can't do such things in *your* business because *your* business is different and *your* clients won't tolerate it. Pfui. It's not like I'm the president or the pope or J-Lo or anybody like that. I'm basically a self-glorified salesman. I've simply done the following three things anyone can do:

1. Decided.
2. Deliberately positioned and marketed myself in a manner conducive to controlling and limiting access.
3. Trained clientele. And they are trainable. When I was a kid, I had litter-box trained pet rabbits that hopped back to their cage to go to the bathroom. I once had a racehorse trained to walk down the barn aisle and turn off the light switches with his mouth. If you can teach a bunny rabbit to go back to his cage to drop doody or a horse to flip light switches, you can train humans to respect you and your time and operate within a few simple rules.

You may or may not want to be as tough as I am. You may not even want to be as tough as many of my clients and Inner Circle Members who've adopted modified versions of my approach. But I will bet you the biggest steak in Texas that you *can* benefit from a tougher screening process than you have now. Think about it.

Fix the Fax

Next, we've got to gain control over and productively use the fax machine. Now let me start by telling you that I'm *not* the world's greatest fan of technology. But I really *love* the fax machine. I think the fax machine is terrific. It's just about my favorite "appliance." (I have no earthly idea how the darned thing works, by the way. It's amazing to me: I stick in a document in Phoenix, push a button, and a fax machine in New Zealand spits it out minutes later. And I thought the self-stick tab on the FedEx envelope was high tech!) Anyway, there are two really good ways to use this magic box to enhance your personal productivity. But, before I tell you about those, let's tackle "the dark side" of this thing—and yes, the fax machine definitely has a "dark side," which I hate.

The Dark Side of Instant Communication

Here's the problem. People who send you faxes think that they've instantly communicated with you and that they should get an immediate response from you. Incredibly, they have this illusion that faxing a document is exactly the same as plunking it into your hands. I guess you're supposed to be sitting there, right next to the fax, watching and waiting. Or that when a fax arrives, everybody's supposed to drop what they are doing, snatch up that fax, burst into your office, interrupt your meeting with the president or the pope, and make you read that fax right now. This attitude was at its worst when faxes were new, but it's still prevalent.

This was and occasionally still is a big problem for me. On a typical day, there will be 20 to 30 to 50 "overnight faxes" waiting, and, during the day, another 20, 30, or more will come zipping in. And remember, I'm not there anyway. So, my beleaguered staff person takes care of the ones she can. The rest get separated into those she judges to be urgent, which get forwarded to me by fax, and those she believes can wait to go in with my week's mail. Even when I was around, I refused to let people pressure me by faxing, I refused to have my day's plan disrupted by faxes, I refused to be controlled by someone else's priorities. So, we have to educate clients about all this.

Since I first penned those above paragraphs about fax, we've added e-mail. Well, I haven't; I won't use that any more than I'll use a cell phone. But *you've* added e-mail. Everything I just said about faxes goes quadruple for e-mail. Listen up: you are not obligated to respond to inbound e-mail instantly, quickly, or ever. I don't need to tell you that if you don't stick a cork in this widening hole, you'll drown trying to handle e-mail. Get tough or die.

With each easier, faster means of communicating, the quantity of dumb, junk communication has multiplied. Because sending an e-mail is so easy and doesn't even require the labor of walking over to the fax machine, people send e-mails any time they have a brain fart. One consultant friend of mine was getting 8 to 20 different, separate e-mails each day from one of his clients—each time the client had a thought or question, zap went the e-mail. In the corporate environment, the individual e-mails have become another Time Vampire trick, a less laborious equivalent of just popping in, standing in the doorway, saying "Got just a minute?"

Again, you may or may not want or need to mirror me. But if you're like many people, and you jump up every time the fax machine beeps, you can't possibly be productive. If somebody runs in to your office every time a fax arrives for you, you're destined for low productivity. If you're checking your e-mail constantly, compulsively, or worse, if you're responding to messages as they arrive—you're headed for an early grave.

For somebody in an office, I think a good system is to take the hour after lunch to look at the morning's faxes, e-mails, and phone calls, deal ONLY with those that are genuinely urgent, and set the others aside. Then, take the last hour of the day to look at the afternoon's accumulated incoming messages, quickly deal with these most urgent and integrate all the rest into your next day's plan. For road warriors, a strategy more like mine may be appropriate.

For far too many people, the phone, the fax machine, e-mail, FedEx—heck, for some people, the mail—invokes a Pavlovian, jump up and instantly respond reaction. If it has never occurred to you before, you ought to look at this now as weird behavior. Who's in charge here anyway? Get a grip.

Finding Power in the Fax

Now, back to ways to use the fax to enhance your productivity. First of all, if you can train your clients, customers, associates, vendors, and others to communicate with you by fax rather than phone, that's a huge productivity advantage. It stops phone tag. It reduces your return call burden. It gets information to you in a more organized way. Often, as people jot out faxes they clarify their own thinking, even answer their own questions. You can deal with these inbounds at your convenience, after hours, while traveling, whatever. When I come home—or if traveling, when I arrive at my hotel—I'd much rather have a stack of faxes than a stack of phone messages. Have you ever gotten a phone message—"Call Bill as soon as you can"—then not been able to reach him and had indigestion after dinner and a sleepless night worrying about what Bill wanted? If Bill had been trained to communicate with you properly by fax, that just wouldn't happen.

Forcing faxes rather than e-mail will also be more productive for you. I've looked at the e-mails people get and compared them to the faxes I get. More thought goes into the faxes. People tend

Incidentally, if YOU want to communicate with me, you can fax me at (602) 269-3113. Just don't sit there holding your breath, waiting for my response.

to cluster multiple items into one fax vs. a stream of single item e-mails. They are more inclined to resolve some things themselves when they must put them into a memo to be faxed than when they can e-mail. The e-mail is more casual, and you really don't want people feeling too casual about consuming your time.

Come to your own conclusions about it all—fax, e-mail, cell. But be the master, not the slave.

Set the Timer on the Bomb

If you do take an incoming call, when you get on the phone with someone, it's a smart idea to set up the exit time first. For example, I'll often say:

> *Tom, I have a conference call starting in just 15 minutes, but I wanted to take your call—I hope that will be enough time for our discussion. Do you agree—or should we set up another telephone appointment?*

Tick, tick, tick.

When someone "drops in," and you decide to go ahead and see them, then, when you bring them into your office, it's a smart idea to set up the exit time first.

Bob, it's difficult these days for me to see drop-in visitors, but it's good to see you. We'll only have half an hour, though, but no longer, as I have an important conference call set for 4:00 P.M. That's OK, isn't it?

Tick, tick, tick.

You may not win any awards for being sociable, but you'll have shorter, more purposeful telephone conversations and meetings. Drop-ins will gradually get the message. Callers will gradually learn to call ahead and set up a phone appointment, or at least, to prepare and be efficient when calling. I call this "setting the timer on the bomb." I even have a clock that looks just like six sticks of dynamite wired together, with a timer on it, and the timer has a flashing red light. This gets a lot of attention plunked down in the center of the conference table. If you're not going to do this physically, you at least want to do it verbally.

You see, *most people will suck up about as much time as you let them.* Salespeople feel productive and satisfied as long as they're talking with customers, and will even extend conversations with a friendly customer as a means of avoiding the risk of confronting new prospects. Employees will dawdle in conversation; it beats working! Conversations have a way of stretching to fill whatever amount of time is available for them.

Be Busy and Be Obvious About It

Obviously busy people are interrupted less than unbusy people. Just like burglars pass up some homes in favor of others, looking for the easiest, safest targets, those who steal and suck up time by interrupting others tend to cruise the office looking for the best opportunity and the easiest target. If you are sitting at your desk, comfortably, appearing relaxed, you're it. Of course, you might be contemplating a formula for disarming a nuclear warhead, but that won't matter, because it's not obvious.

When you are visible to others, it's best to be visibly busy.

CHAPTER 4

The Number One Most
Powerful Personal Discipline
in All the World
And How It Can Make You Successful
Beyond Your Wildest Dreams

There cannot be a crisis next week. My schedule is already full.

—HENRY KISSINGER

I'm sure there are exceptions somewhere, but so far, in 25-plus years of taking note of this, everybody I've met and gotten to know who devoutly adheres to this discipline becomes exceptionally successful AND everybody I've met and gotten to know who ignores this discipline fails. Is it possible that this one discipline alone is so powerful it literally determines success or failure?

The discipline that I am talking about is *punctuality*. Being punctual. Being where you are supposed to be when you are supposed to be there, as promised, without exception, without excuse, every time, all the time. I cannot tell you how important

I believe this is. But I'll tell you some of the reasons why I believe in its indescribably great importance.

First of all, being punctual gives you the right—the positioning—to expect and demand that others treat your time with utmost respect. You cannot reasonably hope to have others treat your time with respect if you show little or no respect for theirs. So, if you are not punctual, you have no leverage, no moral authority. But the punctual person gains that advantage over staff, associates, vendors, clients, everybody.

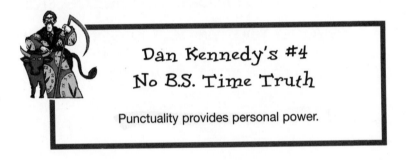

Dan Kennedy's #4
No B.S. Time Truth

Punctuality provides personal power.

The Tragic Case of the Doctor Who Couldn't Tell Time

Some years back, I had a client, a doctor of chiropractic, with a million dollar a year practice and a rather large staff. It was particularly vexing to him that he was unable to rely on any of his staff members to be punctual. Some were habitually late getting to work on time. Others were habitually late getting back from lunch. Others habitually fell behind in getting important paperwork done. And so on. He tried everything—punishments and rewards—and nothing worked. Why? In all the years I knew him, I can't recall this doctor ever getting anywhere on time himself.

He was even 20 minutes late one morning picking me up at my hotel so I could go and teach a time management seminar to his staff! Incredibly, my client never acknowledged the obvious problem here. Maybe there weren't any mirrors in his house.

The Telling Connection Between Punctuality and Integrity

It is my conviction that a person who cannot keep appointments on time, cannot keep scheduled commitments, or cannot stick to a schedule cannot be trusted in other ways either.

Fundamental dishonesty expresses itself in many different ways, but this is definitely one of them. I think it is significant that the man I consider to be the most frequently and consistently dishonest and disreputable U.S. president of my lifetime, Bill Clinton—famous for his tortured deconstruction of the word "is"—was also notorious for being on "Clinton Time"—meaning anywhere from 20 minutes to two hours late to everything, thus being disrespectful to everyone.

There is a link between respect for others' time and respect for others' opinions, property, rights, other kinds of agreements, and contracts. A person reveals a great deal about himself by his punctuality or lack of punctuality. So, as a general rule of thumb, I use this as a means of determining whether or not I want to do business with someone. And, when I violate this, as I occasionally foolishly do, I always get burned.

Let me give you one example: a person seeking to do business with me arranged to meet me at an airport, where I had a 90-minute layover. We agreed, and I confirmed by fax that we would meet at my arrival gate, at my arrival time, and then go to that airline's club room right there on the concourse for the meeting. When I arrived, the guy wasn't there. Some ten minutes later, I'm paged and told to meet him in the main terminal where he is because he ran late getting to the airport. It takes me ten minutes on the tram to get to the main terminal, and I have to cut another ten minutes out of our meeting to allow time to get back to my gate. I have to go through this to meet with a man so disrespectful of a commitment made and of my time that he cannot organize his life to arrive at a meeting on time in his own home city. If he could not be relied on to honor such an easy commitment, why should anybody believe he would honor more important ones?

Still, violating my own rule, I went ahead and accepted this guy as a client. It was predictably ugly. He lied, he cheated, he was completely disorganized, dysfunctional, and unreasonable. He sucked up a pretty good chunk of my time and cost me thousands of dollars to get rid of him. It's not the first time this scenario has taken place in my life. I suppose it won't be the last. But it IS a very reliable principle:

People who can't be punctual, can't be trusted.

For ten years, I appeared 25 to 30 times each year on the number-one speaking tour in America, often addressing audiences of 10,000 to 25,000 people at each event. I was privileged to appear on these programs with many famous speakers, authors, politicians, entertainers, and business leaders, including Paul Harvey, Larry King, the late Coach Tom Landry, Coach Lou Holtz, former Presidents Bush and Ford, Rev. Robert Schuller, "cookie queen" Debbi Fields, Olympians Mary Lou Retton and Bonnie Blair, speakers Zig Ziglar and Tom Hopkins, and the list goes on and on. As the last speaker on a long, full day's program, it was very important to me that the speaker ahead of me stuck to his allotted time and finished on time. It is the professional thing to do. It is respectful to the audience, respectful to the person hiring the speaker, and respectful to the speaker who follows. Most of these speakers understood this and performed accordingly. However, General Colin Powell, who I followed some 40 times, couldn't quite get it done for some reason, typically running 5, 10, or even 15 minutes long—but at least he graciously urged the audience to be sure and stay to hear me. Each year, I sent him a gag-gift clock of one kind or another as a Christmas gift and gentle reminder of "our" little problem.

One time, I spoke after then New York Governor Mario Cuomo at one of these events. He was an unbelievable time hog. He didn't just go 5 or 10 minutes beyond his 45-minute time—he went an unbelievable 20 minutes over! On stage, facing the governor, was a big, digital, red-lighted timer flashing 00:00 after his time ran out, flashing 00:00 for 20 minutes! He ignored it. Staff people signaled him from the side of the stage. He ignored them. I wouldn't trust him as far as I could throw him.

A Simple Way to Favorably Impress Others

Now, here's a "success secret" for you: I'm not the only person to have figured out this punctuality-integrity link. I'm just not *that* smart. I've stumbled on something that a whole lot of other smart, successful, and influential people already know and secretly use to make their determinations about who they will buy from or not buy from, do business with or not do business with, help or not help, trust or distrust. If you are not a punctual person, others you wish to positively influence negatively judge you.

If you think that successful people—people you want to deal with—do not have their own little "systems" for judging people, you're very naive. Not only do they have such a system, most successful people make a point of having "instant reject criteria," to save time in determining who they want to deal with and who they don't.

Just recently, the owner of a printing company was referred to me by a mutual friend. The printing company owner knew we spent a lot of money on printing and was understandably eager to try and get a piece of that business. He came to a meeting prepared with a beautiful portfolio of samples, carefully calculated price proposals, and enthusiastic promises. I sat through it all politely, but I'd made up my mind not to try him out before he even got to the meeting—because he was 20 minutes late getting there. Harsh? Maybe. I'd call it "tough-minded." Getting our printing on time, as scheduled, as promised is critically important. Printed component parts of my products arrive on

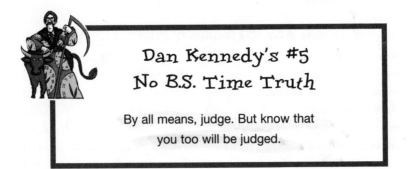

Dan Kennedy's #5 No B.S. Time Truth

By all means, judge. But know that you too will be judged.

Wednesday to be assembled Thursday to ship Friday to a seminar site where I'll be appearing next Tuesday. A day late is as bad as a year late. For a direct-mail campaign, we may have half-a-dozen workers showing up on a given day to assemble sales letters, brochures, and order forms; stuff envelopes; and get out a mailing. If they arrive but the printing doesn't, nothing happens. So when a printer can't get to the first meeting on time, I make the "mental leap" to presuming he can't be relied on to get our jobs done and delivered on time either.

One of my earliest business mentors said that there were only two good reasons for being late for a meeting with him: one, you're dead; two, you want to be.

So, to borrow from Dale Carnegie, if you want to win friends and influence people, be punctual.

And, if you'd like to save yourself a lot of time and trouble, start using this as a means of judging those who would do business with you.

Are Even a Person's Deepest, Darkest Psyche Secrets Revealed by Punctuality?

Punctuality even reveals a lot about an individual's self-esteem. We all know that kids who vandalize other peoples' property for sport, abuse their bodies with drugs, engage in promiscuous, casual, unprotected sex, and otherwise sabotage themselves are, in part, painfully demonstrating low self-esteem. They do not feel that they are important; therefore, no one else and nothing else is very important, and anyone or anything that does seem important is deeply resented. I'd suggest that the adult who does not keep such simple commitments as appointments is not only saying to you that you and your time are unimportant but is unwittingly revealing that he does not feel he and his time are important either. He is, in essence, making a low self-esteem statement.

Some people are deliberately late as a means of trying to be and seem important. Their intended message is: I can keep you waiting because I'm more important than you are. But the message they actually deliver, to those perceptive enough to read behind the lines is: I don't have much self-respect, so I'm desperately trying to make myself feel more like a big shot by stealing your time and getting away with it. Pathetic. And a big, fat warning signal. Deal with this person and you are letting yourself in for all manner of abuse.

CHAPTER 5

The Magic Power that Makes
You Unstoppable

If you're going to do something tonight that you'll be sorry
for tomorrow morning, sleep late.

—COMEDIAN HENNY YOUNGMAN

If I'd known I was going to live this long, I would have taken
better care of myself.

—THE LATE COMEDIAN, PHIL HARRIS

O n the morning of my mother's funeral, I wrote the following paragraph for the original, first edition of this book:

My mother passed away a couple of days, actually nights ago, and the viewing was last night; the memorial service will be in about four hours from now, this morning. It is 6:00 A.M. And here I am, at the keyboard, in my home office, writing. That's what I do almost every day, for at least the first early hour of the morning, no matter what. And that's the answer to how I can have five books in bookstores, a sixth and seventh hitting early in 1996, be under contract for an eighth, for 1997, write my monthly newsletters, and so on.

You can misinterpret, and I realize that. It's not that I'm devoid of emotion, nor that I did not love my mother. However I learned long ago the vital importance of regimen, ritual, commitment, and discipline in relationship to successful achievement. So it takes a lot to derail me. Most people are much, much more easily distracted. Perhaps I'm extreme in my insistence on proceeding with my work plans no matter what, but most people are even more extreme in their willingness to set aside their work plans for just about anything—hangnail, stiff breeze.

How a "Little Man" Reminds Us of "The Magic Power" 8,000 Times and Counting

Some of you may know that I'm a horse racing aficionado. For me, a bad day at the track beats a good day at the office. I could relate when George Burns as God in the movie *Oh God!* headed off to the track with a racing form stuck in his back pocket to watch "the magnificent animals I created. I did very good work there." The racetrack is one of the most interesting places on earth. And there, like everywhere we really look, we can find powerful reminders of what it takes to excel in this world.

At age 46, Laffit Pincay, Jr., had accomplished just about everything a jockey can hope to accomplish. He had won the Kentucky Derby, the Belmont, six Breeder's Cups, the Eclipse Award five times, and he had already been in the Sports Hall of Fame—for 18 years. In 1995, he won his 8,000th race. He has since retired at age 56.

A decade ago, you wouldn't have found any racing authority who would have bet that Pincay would still be riding, winning, and winning more frequently than most, at the old-for-athletes age of 46, and on to 50. To a man, we would all have bet against

Pincay. It is one thing for a Nolan Ryan to have defied age in baseball. For Jerry Rice to defy age in football. But as a jockey, Pincay had to somehow keep his weight to 115 pounds. His frame would ordinarily have carried 140 and, with age, as we all seem to do, take on 10, 20, even 30 more pounds in that spare tire around the waist. But Pincay stayed at 115.

For most, the mental strain of this would prove impossible. Pincay probably learned more about nutrition, weight loss, and diet than anybody—because he had to. He had to know precisely how many calories and fat grams were in each bite of food he swallowed. When preparing his own meals, he had to measure each portion to the ounce. There was a book-length list of foods he could NEVER eat. To satisfy his taste buds, to fool his taste buds, he sometimes chewed on a piece of cake or other "sweet," but then spit it out like a wad of chewing tobacco. Everyday, every meal, he had to exercise rigid self-control. At his age, if he slipped and gained a pound, he might never get rid of it.

Most days, Laffit Pincay put on a warm-up suit and speed-walked the track where he was racing, clockwise, at a time of day before he had to get ready to ride but as late in the morning as possible so as to take full advantage of the hot sun's ability to burn off any excess fluids in his body. He had a strict, demanding, daily exercise regimen. And ounce for ounch, inch for inch, he may have been the best conditioned athlete in America. Pincay's body fat percentage was, well, so near zero it wasn't worth measuring. He had the upper body of a weight lifter. His thigh muscles rivaled Schwarzenegger at his prime. A famous orthopedist involved in sports medicine described him as a perfect miniature replica of an NFL linebacker.

And let's remember that this "little fellow" climbed up on and controlled 1,000-pound beasts. If you watch Thoroughbred

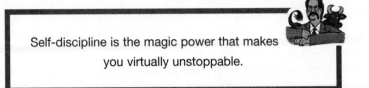

Self-discipline is the magic power that makes
you virtually unstoppable.

horse racing, you'll quickly see that this is no easy task. Perched
like a bird on top of an elephant, the jockey cannot control the
horse through brute strength. There is that, but there is more. A
horse either respects his jockey or he does not. Most respected
Pincay. A 115-pound embodiment of extraordinary, applied self-
discipline that commanded respect from beast as well as man.

How to Make the World Hand Over Just about Anything You Ask

Having and commanding the respect of others is a tremendous
advantage in life. That edge comes from self-discipline. Having a
(preferably private) sense of superiority over others is another
power-producing edge. That, too, comes from self-discipline.
The highly disciplined individual does not have to point a gun at
anyone to take what he wants; people "sense" his power and
cheerfully give him everything they've got.

Take a look at how little discipline most people have. I admit,
I couldn't match Lafitt Pincay. One of America's greatest humor-
ous speakers, Charlie Jarvis, tells of coming home from a trip and
confessing to his wife that he'd violated his diet and wolfed
down a Snickers bar at the airport snack shop. After she chided
him, he pointed out that he had actually demonstrated enormous
self-discipline: "I wanted to wolf down ALL the Snickers bars."
I'm sorry to say, I was in that category more often than not for

years. Still, compared to most of the people I observe, I was a self-discipline master even then. These days, I must control what I eat much more carefully than ever. I peeled off 45 pounds from my heaviest peak; I keep that off and my diabetes in check without prescription medication of any kind. I must pay attention to carb counts and blood sugar levels, and I take about 50 different vitamin, mineral, and herbal supplements a day. Compare that to the average "wide-load" American, who can't go a full day resisting junk food. In 2003, a record number of "million-dollar babies" in the NFL showed up at camp overweight and out of shape.

I have noticed, since I took off my fat and got my physical condition under better control, my income has gone up. Is this coincidental? Maybe. Complex? Maybe. But quite probably it reflects an unconscious preference on clients' part to have confidence in, to trust, to give money to, to meet the fee demands without question of someone who appears to have self-esteem, self-control, self-discipline. Food—pardon the word—for thought.

As I was writing the first edition of this book, a young lady named Shannon Faulkner concluded a two-year court battle in order to gain entrance to the all-male military academy, The Citadel. Her presence there was bitterly opposed by the administration, faculty, students, and alumni. On her day of arrival, armed guards escorted her in. One week later, she quit. Setting all political arguments aside, I believe that she or some woman in her position could have won the grudging respect of a significant number of the other cadets, won over some, made allies, and gotten through the academy—but, incredibly, with two years to prepare, knowing that such a military academy features tough physical as well as mental activity, knowing she would be put upon—she showed up more than 20 pounds overweight and clearly in no condition to withstand the rigors of the physical training. On the first 100-degree day, Faulkner wound up in the clinic with heat stroke. To be fair, four male cadets went with her. But many more didn't. And she couldn't afford to. If she had possessed the self-discipline to thoroughly prepare for what was obviously going to be a physical and emotional ordeal, she could have earned the respect of enough people there to, first, survive; second, gradually thrive; and overall, succeed. But in America these days, people don't think they should have to *earn* anything anymore. They feel entitled.

Take a look at how little self-discipline most people have. The thousands of business owners I work with tell me more than half their rank-and-file workers frequently show up late for work. Ask any employer of size and you'll hear how big the problems of tardiness and absenteeism are. People do not even have enough self-discipline to get up in the morning! It seems that the majority of today's work force cannot cannot be depended on to read, write, count, or to do anything on their own to improve their skills. (Which is why they are replaced by automation, relocation of jobs to foreign lands, and through every other means possible.)

In my business dealings, I find more than half the people cannot seem to get to appointments and meetings on time or keep preset telephone appointments. Clients miss pre-scheduled coaching appointments. Vendors miss deadlines as often as they make them.

Woody Allen once observed half of success seems to be showing up. Ed Foreman, a popular motivational speaker, very successful businessman, and, I think, the only man to be elected to Congress representing two different states at two different times, says you can be certain of rapid advancement in most business organizations if you'll just do three things:

1. Show up.
2. Show up on time.
3. Show up on time, ready to work. So few do.

Lafitt Pincay, Jr., never failed to show up, show up on time, 110% ready to give each ride his very best effort.

In the entrepreneurial environment, it is much the same. There's a lot to be said just for showing up on time, ready to work. (Not hung over. Not exhausted. Not distracted.) The meeting of deadlines and commitments alone causes a person to stand out from the crowd like an alien space ship parked in an Iowa cornfield. The ability to get things done and done right the first time will magnetically attract incredible contacts, opportunities, and resources to you. All of this is a matter of self-discipline.

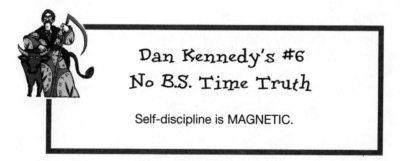

Dan Kennedy's #6
No B.S. Time Truth

Self-discipline is MAGNETIC.

And self-discipline aimed and applied at a particular thing, as I do to writing, as Pincay does to fitness, is quite literally a magic power. When you focus your self-discipline on a single purpose, like sunlight through a magnifying glass on a single object, look out! The whole world will scramble to get out of your way, hold the doors open for you, and salute as you walk by.

The Inextricable Link between Time Management and Self-Discipline

It takes tremendous self-discipline to productively allocate and invest time and to stick to your intentions. It's said that "the road to hell is paved with good intentions," and I believe it. Although some people find it hard to believe, I'm one of the laziest guys on the planet. There's no internal force that drives me to work. Every morning, I have a little fight with myself, and I have to force myself to haul it out of bed and into the office. On the road, I may sit on the edge of the bed and glare at my laptop and battle with my lazy self to do what I need to do. And I could quite happily forget it all, go find a hammock on the beach, and sleep all day long.

I think this is a secret true of a lot of very successful people. I think they are secretly lazy and become exceptionally self-disciplined out of necessity.

Because the entrepreneur is his own boss and can do as he pleases with his time, it is very important to be self-disciplined. The entrepreneur with a loose, buddy-buddy, easily forgiving boss will never accomplish much. It is the entrepreneur with the tough taskmaster as a boss who excels.

"Success Leaves Clues"

Tony Robbins says, "Success leaves clues." It seems that the Creator thought it a good idea to leave clues to success all over the place, so that—if you have your eyes open—you can't stand in any one place, turn all the way around, and not find one. You can go to the racetrack, of all places, and find clues. You can watch sports on TV and find clues. You can pick up a magazine and find clues. You can drive down a street and look at the businesses and see clues.

The one thing that seems universal is that self-discipline is evident in every winner.

The great success educator Earl Nightingale once said that if you couldn't find a heroic, successful role model, then just look at what everybody else is doing and don't do that. Look at how everybody else behaves and do the opposite. It turns out that this is good advice for salespeople and businesspeople, but it would also be very good advice to kids stuck growing up in a ghetto or newly elected politicians in Washington.

When you look around at what I call The Mediocre Majority, you'll find that the one thing that appears universal with them is the lack of self-discipline.

CHAPTER 6

The Ten Time
Management Techniques
Really Worth Using

I'm going to graduate on time, no matter how long it takes.
—SENIOR BASKETBALL PLAYER, UNIVERSITY OF PITTSBURGH

M y business—*the information business*, as well as businesses such as weight loss, diet, and financial advisory services—revolves around the public's stubborn belief that there must be a "secret" to success, concealed from them, possibly by conspiracy, that if uncovered, would change everything. This concept can be useful to remember if you work in advertising, marketing, and selling, but it is a useless, even harmful, delusion otherwise. With regard to time, I promise you, there's no secret magic pill you don't know about. And no new, whiz-bang, computerized doohickey or color-coded appointment book is going to change everything.

54

In business, there are good strategies poorly executed, poor strategies executed well, but rarely is there a truly new, revolutionary strategy. In this chapter are ten good strategies. Nothing earth-shaking, nothing revolutionary, probably nothing you don't already know. The issue is execution, not innovation.

The "joke" in the weight-loss industry, where I find myself doing marketing consulting from time to time, is this: if there were a diet that worked, there'd only be one diet. Similarly, you could reasonably argue that if there was one time management system that worked perfectly for everybody, there'd be only one system. The good news is that, in a way, there IS just one time management "system," and it's all here in this chapter.

If you read every time management book ever written, go to every time management seminar offered, and, more importantly, observe and analyze lots of people who get an exceptional quantity of important things accomplished, you will be able to boil ALL the technique "stuff" down to only ten things worth doing. So, let me save you all that time and just hand them to you here. I'll note, too, that all ten might not apply to you and your situations. When it's all said and done, you sort of have to find your own way.

Technique #1: Tame the Phone

As I discussed in detail elsewhere in this book, you've got to free yourself from the tyranny of the phone. And the fax. And e-mail. And similar stuff. Take few if any incoming calls. Return your calls at your convenience. As this is the number-one source of disruption and distraction for most people, you must get a firm grip on this technique.

Technique #2: Minimize Meetings

Find every way possible to minimize your time spent in formal meetings. Most meetings end where they begin anyway.

I deal with one company where literally every time I call, anyone I call is always "in a meeting." The company has six conference rooms—a very bad sign. If Noah had convened a meeting of architects, interior decorators, goat and sheep herders, lion tamers, navigators, we would all have fins. Nothing ever got done in a meeting. I hate 'em.

For a lot of people, meetings are a place to hide out. Or preen and be important. But not a place to actually do work or get anything done. You need a strategy to avoid them. If you lead meetings, you need a strategy to abbreviate and focus them. If you must attend meetings, you need a strategy to escape from them at will.

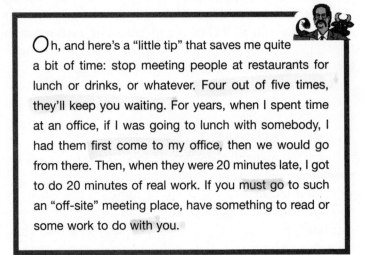

Oh, and here's a "little tip" that saves me quite a bit of time: stop meeting people at restaurants for lunch or drinks, or whatever. Four out of five times, they'll keep you waiting. For years, when I spent time at an office, if I was going to lunch with somebody, I had them first come to my office, then we would go from there. Then, when they were 20 minutes late, I got to do 20 minutes of real work. If you must go to such an "off-site" meeting place, have something to read or some work to do with you.

Technique #3: Practice Absolute Punctuality
See Chapter 4.

Technique #4: Make and Use Lists
There is not a single time management discipline or system on earth that doesn't revolve around making and using lists. You CANNOT carry it all in your head. For years, I've operated with four basic lists:

1. *My Schedule.* This is for the entire year, day by day.
2. *Things to Do List.* My basic "Things to Do" list is organized by the month, the week, and each day, prioritized as A's, B's, and C's. Management consultant (and "hustler") Ivy Lee reportedly sold this idea to billionaire industrialist Andrew Carnegie's right-hand man, Charles Schwab, for $25,000.00. It worked for Schwab. It works for just about everybody who uses it now.
3. *People to Call List.* My third list is a "People to Call" list, also prioritized alphabetically.
4. *Conference Planner.* And finally, I have the "Conference Planner"—just a page for each person I interact with a lot, where I jot down things I need to talk to them about as they occur to me in between meetings or conversations.

To be perfectly honest, I do this with a yellow legal pad and pages I most often carry folded up in my pocket. And I'll admit that this is not exactly a shining example for a time management "leader" to set, but I've found that this works just as well for me as a number of different, more organized and formal systems I've tried. Over the years, I've experimented with the Day-Timer and

Incidentally, if you are a "free spirit," you might think something like these lists to be intolerably confining, like a pair of jockey shorts mistakenly bought one size too small. (What?—like I'm the only one to ever make that mistake.) Actually, once you get used to using these lists, you'll find them mentally, creatively liberating. Why? Because the more details you get on paper, the fewer you must remember and worry about remembering. This frees your mind up for more important tasks.

several other systems, even one I designed myself. Anyway, the "magic" is more in the making and using the lists than in the particular tool, media, or format you use.

I also use a "storyboard" for planning, somewhat like the storyboard used to plan a TV program or movie. My speaking colleague Mike Vance, author of *Think Outside the Box*, teaches this method. As I've had Mike speak twice to my Inner Circle Members in past years, quite a few of my Members and clients have learned this and use it, reporting great results.

I'm usually amused by people dependent on their Palm Pilot devices and laptops for their schedules, plans, and lists. On more than one occasion, I've heard them wailing about the machine gleefully erasing everything and leaving them with a blank screen. Or watched their batteries go dead. So far, the tri-folded pages in my jacket pocket and pen have not failed me.

Ultimately, though, whether with crayon and pad or computer, you have got to get some sort of regimented, regularly used list-making system working for you. If you aren't making lists, you probably aren't making a lot of money either.

Technique #5: Fight to Link Everything to Your Goals
(The secret reason why there aren't more millionaires)

My speaking colleague Jim Rohn often says that the only real reason more people do not become millionaires is that they don't have enough reasons to. It's certainly not lack of opportunity! Look around. You can't pick up a magazine without reading of people who've taken very ordinary ideas, even weird ideas, and used them to become rich. You can't pick up a magazine and not read of someone who has scrambled up out of poor circumstances and gotten rich. So why don't more people become millionaires? They just don't have enough reasons to.

Similarly, I insist that the only real reason more people aren't much, much more productive is that they don't have enough reasons to. So, a secret to greater personal productivity is more good reasons to be more productive. That's why you have to fight to link everything you do (and choose not to do) to your goals.

Frankly, this is very difficult. You've undoubtedly heard the adage: when you're up to your neck in alligators, it's difficult to remember that your original objective was to drain the swamp. And, having been up to my neck in alligator-filled swamp water more often than I like to remember, I know just how tough it is to keep at least one eye fixed firmly on your list of goals. But that's EVERYTHING. That is what gets goals achieved. And that is what creates peak productivity, as I'll explain.

In the 1980s, "productivity" was a big, big buzzword. There were all sorts of folks running around teaching businesses and businesspeople every conceivable gimmick for improving productivity—without ever defining or (I contend) knowing what the heck productivity was. For corporations, there was regurgitated Demingism, Japanese management styles, MBO, MBV, and on and on. All in search of an invisible, ill-defined intangible.

If you're going to achieve peak personal productivity, you've got to *define* peak personal productivity.

Here's an old joke: the wife prevails upon her husband, an avid hunter, to take her along on the annual deer hunting trip, so she can finally see what all the fuss is about. To keep her out of harm's way, he stations her at the bottom of a hill and instructs her to shoot her gun into the air as a signal if she spots deer. Then he and the other guys head off through the woods, toward the creek, where deer are likely to be found. About ten minutes later, they hear not one but four quick shots. They race back to the hill, where the wife is standing, pointing her rifle at a fellow standing next to a fallen, dead horse. The guy is saying, "OK lady, it's your deer. But at least let me get my saddle."

If you don't know what peak personal productivity looks like, how are you gonna hit it?

So, here's my definition:

Note that this definition presupposes the existence of meaningful goals. I don't know of a single successful individual, in

> P roductivity is the deliberate, strategic investment of your time, talent, intelligence, energy, resources, and opportunities in a manner calculated to move you measurably closer to meaningful goals.

any field, who isn't goal-directed, and who is not involved in measuring, preferably daily, movement toward those goals. Paul Meyer, founder of Success Motivation Institute, once stated that, if you are not achieving what you feel you should in life, it is because your goals are not defined well enough. But my definition of productivity goes beyond that. It says that you cannot be productive without goals, in fact, without linkage with goals. It says you cannot be productive without *measurement.*

This gives you a very simple standard for determining, minute by minute, task by task, choice by choice, whether you are being productive or unproductive:

> *Is what I am doing, this minute, moving me measurably closer to my goals?*

Now, to be reasonable, and to be human, let's cheerfully acknowledge that nobody can—or should—be able to say "yes" to that question all of the time. We need, want, and deserve time for casual conversation, for baseball scores, for political arguments, for reading the comics, for just plain goofing off. But you want to do those things knowingly, consciously, by choice, not by random accident or others' direction.

I'd say that anything beyond a 50% "yes rate" qualifies as peak personal productivity. Incidentally, measurement alone will enhance your productivity. Just asking the question will enhance your productivity. Any athlete will tell you that measurement alone improves performance.

Technique #6: Tickle the Memory with Tickler Files

I've got a memory like a steel trap. A rusted steel trap. Seems a lot seeps out through those rust holes. For example, I seem to have mental blocks about how old people are (the ONLY person's age I know is mine), birthdays, anniversaries, holidays, peoples' names. With this in mind, I wrote a country-western song: *I Love My Wife But I Can't Remember Where I Live*. Perversely, I can perfectly recall the lyrics from 20-year-old songs, obscure actors' names, and a collection of other useless trivia. If I could remember to phrase it as a question, I'd go on *Jeopardy!* and get rich. Seriously, I need tools and systems to substitute for memory. The Tickler File is one of my favorites.

The more I use this technique, the better I like it, although it does work much better for someone who gets to his desk everyday than for someone as mobile as I. The idea is simple: you have 90 file folders: numbered 1 through 30; blue numbered 1 through 30; and white 1 through 30 representing the current month, next month and the month after that. This is most commonly used by accountant-type folks, to keep track of bills to be paid. (We use it for that purpose in our office.) But it can be used for anything. Let's assume you agree to follow up with a client on a particular matter on the tenth of next month. Take either that client's whole file or just that piece of correspondence or just a handwritten note and plop it into the Blue file folder numbered 10. And forget it. On the 10th of next month, it'll pop up all by itself and remind you to do it. Used right, these Tickler Files reduce clutter, serve as automatic memory, and help organize daily activities.

Yes, I know there are all sorts of "contact management programs" for desktop and laptop computers that do this same thing, and if you want to go that way, by all means, be my guest. For me, though, this would be one of those examples of using technology just because the technology exists, not because it's better. Running my Tickler Files on my laptop would require me to input or scan in stuff needlessly, and it still wouldn't accommodate the "lumpy stuff," like a whole client file or a 56-page infomercial proposal or, well, you get the idea. But whether you choose manual or automated, this is a very good technique.

Technique #7: Block Your Time

Here is one of the real, hidden secrets of people who consistently achieve peak productivity: make inviolate appointments with yourself. You know, we all do a pretty good job at keeping the appointments we make with others. We have this skill down. So, why not use it to get things done?

I am completing this book in December. As of the writing of this edition of this book, my calendar for next year has nine days assigned to doing tele-coaching sessions with 45 Gold/VIP Members, 22 days to mastermind meetings with VIP and Platinum groups, eight travel days related to those meetings, five speaking engagement days, three travel days for those, and ten days of pre-arranged vacations. That's 57 of 365 blocked. Then there are holidays, a couple of birthdays, Super Bowl Sunday, that sort of thing, another ten. Only 298 days remain available. But that's still a lot of days to wander and meander around in. The less wandering and meandering the better. The more time gets blocked, the less room there is to aimlessly meander. So I also go ahead and block out the times I'll record my monthly tapes for Gold Members, the days I'll use to write my newsletter, other reoccurring activities. On a week-to-week basis, I block the morning hours when I write and the Monday and Wednesday evenings when I drive in harness races. For the year, for the quarter immediately ahead, for the month ahead, and week ahead, I try to leave as little "loose" or unassigned time as possible. Then I treat the blocked times—even those that are work appointments or play appointments with myself—just as inviolate as I do a paid speaking gig or consulting day.

One of the things I'm asked most often about my own work habits is how I manage to do so much writing along with everything else I do. Just to quickly tick these things off, during the year I speak, spend 30 or 40 single days of consulting with new clients, service two dozen or so consulting clients at any one time, attend several major multi-day conventions, run my own publishing and mail-order business, and attend other business interests, investments, and my racing activities. Then on top of all that, I write at least one book a year for trade publishers that go into the bookstores, edit two monthly newsletters, and do a tremendous amount of advertising copywriting for my clients. How do I do all that writing?

There are two answers. First, I write for at least one hour every morning, virtually no matter what. The first hour of my morning, sometimes 5:00 to 6:00, often 6:00 to 7:00, occasionally 7:00 to 8:00, I write. At home, on the road, doesn't matter. Weekdays or weekends, doesn't matter. Tired or not, doesn't matter. Inspired or not, doesn't matter. If I am under a tough copywriting deadline for a client, I'll give the hour to that task. Most days, that first hour goes to my own books, tapes, and newsletters. Second, I block time often weeks and occasionally months in advance, as appointments with myself for certain writing projects. If I did not "block time" this way, I assure you, I'd get a fraction of this output done, and I'd be woefully behind all the time.

In short, if you lay your calendar out before you and pre-assign or block as much of your time as possible, as much in advance as possible—carved in rock not written lightly in pencil—you will

S ome years back, I was counseling a chiropractor new to practice and advised her to close her office for one day a week, call that "Marketing Day," and devote that entire day to calling patients, visiting health-food stores, calling on businesses, giving speeches, and so on. Left to be "fit in" as time allowed, most of these very productive things would never have happened.

then leave yourself only a small amount of loose, unassigned time. Further, by blocking time for important, high-value functions you perform, you prevent demands of others from moving your highest and best-value activities from number one to number ten on your list, over and over again.

Technique #8: Minimize Unplanned Activity

By reducing unscheduled time and unplanned activity, you automatically reduce waste.

If you look around carefully, you'll see that most people just sort of show up. They arrive at the office and react. If you press them for their day's plan, you'll find they may have only one or two scheduled activities—one of which is usually lunch. (That attitude reminds me of the *Peanuts* cartoon: what class do you like best? Recess.) They may also have a few things on a "loose" things-to-do list. All the unscheduled time somehow gets used up, but if you again press them at the end of the day, or better yet, at the end of the week, they cannot tell you where it went.

Just as the person who cannot tell you where his money goes is forever destined to be poor, the person who cannot tell you where his time goes is forever destined to be unproductive. And, often, poor.

Ideally, you should schedule your day by the half-hour, from beginning to end.

If you do project work as I do, it's important to estimate the minutes or hours required and work against the clock, against deadlines. Every task gets completed faster and more efficiently when you have determined in advance how long it should take and set a time for its completion. This, too, minimizes unplanned activity.

Technique #9: Profit from "Odd-Lot" Time

Stuck in traffic? Audiocassette tapes and CDs—arguably the greatest educational inventions since the Gutenberg press—let you easily and cheaply turn your car into a classroom, a seminar with America's best speakers, an uplifting literary experience, a laugh-filled comedy club, or a Shakespearean festival. Just about every notable self-improvement, sales training, marketing or business expert, author or speaker has a variety of material available in audio form. (For a catalog of mine, log onto www.dankennedyproducts.com.) But you needn't stop there. Information about any and every topic, from experts ranging from noted college professors to nutrition, health, and fitness gurus to, well, you name it, is available in audio form. Books on tape or CD provide great readings and condensations of every-thing from the greatest literature of all time to the most contem-porary novels. If you need some endorphin therapy, pick up copies of the great radio comedies of old, or famous comics like Bob and Ray, or very current stand-up comedians. Or learn a foreign language, improve your memory, improve your math skills, all by plugging in a cassette tape or CD during otherwise wasted time.

Waiting time in offices, airports? Take along a cassette or CD player and an earplug or a file of magazines and newsletters to go through at your convenience. Keep handy a notepad, a pen, and a topic to think about and brainstorm. Have mini-projects and throw-away reading with you or Psycho-Cybernetics mental exercises to do (for more information see Chapter 12). As they say in Washington, a billion here, a billion there, pretty soon you're spending real money. Well, five minutes here, ten minutes there, and pretty soon you're wasting hours.

Technique #10: Live Off Peak

Why make life more difficult than it already is?

There are obvious ways to use this technique. For example, avoid going to the bank on Fridays, especially after 11:00 A.M., and especially if it is the 1st or 15th of the month. Avoid going to the supermarket the day before a holiday weekend. Avoid going to the post office the day after a rate increase (an unfortunately increasingly common occurrence).

I suppose everybody knows these things. But there are many similar patterns and instances of "herd behavior" that you can avoid. In Phoenix, where I lived for 24 years, I could drive from my home to my office in ten minutes if I did it after 9:00 A.M., but it took a half hour or more if I tried it between 7:30 and 8:30 A.M. Thanks to the idiotic refusal by the Phoenix authorities to install left turn arrows, it was often easier, faster, and safer to make three right turns and go around a block than to wait in line and make one left turn.

On the road, I try to avoid having to check out and leave a hotel between 8:00 and 9:00 A.M. or checking in between 4:00 and 6:00 P.M., because that's when everybody else checks in and out. When you take note of these things and organize your life to work around them, you can save a lot of time and avoid a lot of frustration.

CHAPTER 7

How to Turn Time into Wealth

There is only one success—to be able to spend your life in your own way.

—CHRISTOPHER MORLEY

For every action, there is an equal or opposite criticism.

—AUTHOR UNKNOWN

There is an old joke that says: "I've been rich and I've been poor. Rich is definitely better." Well, I concur. I make absolutely no apology for striving to be rich and for teaching and inspiring others to do the same. Furthermore, I believe you have every right to figure out ways to make maximum money from minimum time. When you can honestly apply the axiomatic advice of "work smarter, not harder," more power to you! I do not think any special heroism comes from earning your money through back-breaking work or long hours.

My Platinum Member Ron LeGrand, who has bought and "flipped" thousands of properties and teaches his real estate profit methods to thousands of investors each year, has a pet saying:

"The less I do, the more I make." It is obviously open to misinterpretation. Ron works and does so cheerfully. But he has learned to focus on work that directly produces wealth.

I suspect I am unique in working up close, personal, hands-on with more than 100 first-generation millionaire and multimillionaire entrepreneurs, most of whom built their wealth by creating and building new businesses from scratch, many of whom hit the million-dollar mark in a hurry. I have been in their offices, they in mine; had hundreds of hours of telephone conversations with them; worked with them individually and in groups; and had countless opportunities over years to observe their behavior and probe their psyches. My Renegade Millionaire System and once-a-year seminar I hold deal exclusively and extensively with what separates these "renegade millionaires" from the pack. (For more information about my system and seminars, go to www.renegademillionaire.com.) One of the key factors in their success is the way they link time to money, and think in terms of investing time. Most, like Ron, are always looking for ways to get more for less, invest fewer minutes of work, extract more dollars.

One way they do this is by making themselves into bona fide experts in some field, one thing from which wealth can come. There is the old story about the customer angrily demanding an itemized bill from the plumber, who submitted a $250.00 bill for two minutes' work—smacking the clogged pipe with a hammer. The plumber wrote out the itemized bill as follows: For hitting pipe with hammer: $5.00. For knowing where to hit pipe with hammer: $245.00. Getting into that position—when you can be paid not (just) for what you do (physical labor) but for what you know (intellectual equity)—is a very worthy objective.

So, let there be no mistake. I think you deserve to be rich. I think you have a right to be rich. I think you provide enormous service to society by getting and being rich. I think government should be forbidden from penalizing or attacking you for being rich.

"On the Other Hand . . ."

With all that said, though, I have to suggest that money isn't everything.

It is a lot easier to give the "money isn't everything" and "money doesn't buy happiness" lecture after you have a considerable amount of money than before. Personally, I always resented hearing it when I was broke. And believe me, I understand that a person NEEDS a certain level of financial success before he can give a great deal of thought to the bigger philosophical issues of life. And I think in our land of great opportunity, it is disgraceful not to do well. I don't see any honor in being poor. No shame in it as a temporary condition but there should be shame if being poor is accepted as a permanent way of life. But, to be certain, money is only part, and maybe a small part, of "wealth."

On a surprisingly cool summer morning in Cleveland, Ohio, I sit in a dirty jog cart (the work-a-day version of a sulky), reins in hands, bouncing along behind an aging, mildly lame, Standardbred horse on the Northfield Park backstretch. Damp dirt, gravel, and bits of manure are kicked up past the mud screen onto my boots and pants, occasionally hitting my face. I am in seventh heaven. Of course, I'm just fooling around. But most of the folks there doing the same thing and taking care of these horses as work are in seventh heaven too. They couldn't imagine doing anything else. On this particular day and night, a 70-year-old man, Earl Bowman, and his wife, Joanna, were celebrating their 50th wedding anniversary. Earl, a retired driver and still a very good trainer, took his horse to the paddock, took care of it and worked just as he would any other night. After the race, Joanna joined him as he led the horse into the winners' circle for the photo. Then he took the horse back to the barns where he had another hour's work ahead of him, stripping off the harness, bathing the horse, walking the horse to cool him out, bandaging the horse's legs, and so on. And if you asked Earl if he could have gone anywhere else or done anything else on that night, what would he wish for, he'd have no answer. *This* is wealth.

On a Thursday afternoon, General Norman Schwarzkopf finishes his speech on leadership; the emcee quickly introduces me; I step to the stage in The Palace in Auburn Hills, Michigan, where the Detroit Pistons play basketball; I address more than 20,000 people for an hour and then answer questions and sign autographs. When all the dust settles, I earn about $25,000.00 from the audience's purchases of my books and tapes. A few weeks later in Phoenix, I have 22 people in a three-day seminar, each paying $2,500.00 to be there, and I talk to them about my favorite subject: direct marketing. I and the group "brainstorm" each attendee's business and project. In these situations, I'm having a ball. It definitely beats REALLY working for a living! *This* is wealth.

Many days, I get paid handsomely to consult with interesting people, one on one, and help them figure out the best answers to their marketing problems. Other days, I sit at my computer and create powerful sales letters and marketing documents for my clients or my own products. Or I write newsletters, articles, and books like this one. I enjoy every minute of it. *This* is wealth.

A Wealthy Man

In South Bend, Indiana, one of the brightest, most interesting, most generous, most spiritual men I know, Dr. Herb True, teaches a management class at Notre Dame in the afternoon. Then he rushes home, takes phone calls from students, briefly visits with his wife, Betty, gathers up a slide presentation, and goes to the Center for the Homeless, where every Monday night, he conducts classes on humor (yes, humor!), self-esteem, hope, faith, and love. Early in his career, Herb taught at Notre Dame, but then he left, went into the "real world," and became one of the most successful and sought-after professional speakers in America. In 1982, he set aside his very lucrative speaking career and returned to Notre Dame to work with young people and give his time to his community. The pay cut he took is, well, epic. These days, he still accepts a couple dozen speaking engagements from companies that pursue him, but he donates all the fees to the homeless centers in South Bend. Herb is 71 years young. He works harder than he ever did. Although he lives in the same very modest home he has lived in for decades, although he does not drive a new car, although his annual income is nothing to brag about, Herb is a very, very wealthy man.

The individual who gets to use his time in ways that bring him great joy and fulfillment, who gets to do work that is genuinely personally interesting, who gets to choose his associates, and who gets to make some kind of a contribution to his fellow man wakes up wealthy every morning and goes to bed wealthy every night, regardless of his bank balance.

I do not happen to believe in the vow-of-poverty approach. To the contrary, I favor making very good money. But, unlike some "motivational speakers" insistent on telling everybody they *should* pursue millions of dollars, I've long been willing to acknowledge that these things have different meanings for different people. You do not necessarily need a million dollars in the bank or a huge home on the hill or Jay Leno's fleet of expensive cars in order to be wealthy. Many people manage to get rich, but comparatively few get wealthy. As long as you're going to put in your time on the planet, why not invest it in a way that makes you *wealthy*?

Napoleon Hill, most famous for his classic best-selling book, *Think and Grow Rich*, spent his entire life encouraging people to pursue great goals, including financial riches. Hill was originally set out on his mission by America's first billionaire, Andrew Carnegie, who believed there were "universal principles of success" that could be taught and learned, just as any other collection of mechanical skills could be learned. Carnegie helped get Hill in-depth interviews and relationships with hundreds of the greatest achievers of that era. Hill identified 13 commonalties, and wrote about them, first in *The Laws of Success*, then in *Think and Grow Rich*. Following publication of that book in 1937, Napoleon Hill lectured, trained large sales organizations, recorded inspirational messages, and, in various ways, distributed his "science of success" based on those 13 principles.

Late in his life, Napoleon Hill wrote another book I highly recommend: *Grow Rich with Peace of Mind*. In this book, after acquiring great riches, losing great riches, and a long career, Napoleon Hill did his best to reconcile the issues of pursuing great financial success and achieving total wealth, in the bigger, broader sense.

How Much Is Enough?

So, how do you turn time into wealth? Reverse engineering. Decide what "wealth" means to you. This includes what I call your "enough is enough number"—the total of investable assets you need to feel secure and spin off sufficient income to support you and your family as you wish to live. Not at wild-fantasy, win-the-lottery, own-a-castle-in-Spain levels, at least not for most people, but a reasonable yet desirable level. Develop a clear, detailed picture of what your life would look like and how you would live if you had that "number" in place. Does this picture include a second home or a big vacation twice a year or owning a bed-and-breakfast? In this picture, how do you use, spend, and invest your time?

Once you have this entire picture built, with detailed clarity, you can begin looking backward, to where you are now. You identify the obstacles in the path and begin looking for and thinking about all the possible ways they might be removed. You can construct a plan. Establish yearly, monthly, weekly targets and benchmarks. Then, most important of all, you can judge whether your present moment's choices made with your time are linked to creating the wealth you desire.

CHAPTER 8

On the Road Again.
I Just Can't Wait to Get
on the Road Again.

When two trains approach each other at a crossing, they shall
both come to a full stop and neither shall start up until
the other has gone.

—A LAW IN KANSAS, FROM THE BOOK *THE 776 STUPIDEST THINGS EVER SAID*
BY ROSS AND KATHRYN PETRAS

Yech. I am a reluctant road warrior. For more than ten years, I averaged more than 100 days a year on the road. I liked what I did when I got there, but I didn't like anything about the getting there. And this dislike grew day by day. Throughout my peak travel years, I was inspired to be as efficient as possible about travel, as productive as possible while traveling. Each time I grumblingly got onto an airplane, I wanted that trip to be as valuable as possible. That's what I'll talk with you about in this chapter: how to travel for business with as much productivity as possible. But I do want to be totally honest about this—in the post 9-11 world, the problems and agony have exponentially multiplied. Long before 9-11, I was well on my way to slashing my business travel, and now travel less than in any of the prior 15 years.

As an aside, I believe a law should be passed requiring every airline executive, on his birthday, to go out to dinner, to his favorite restaurant, with family and friends. While the rest of the party can order anything they choose from the menu, the executive will get a standard airline dinner. After he gets frisked. And he has to eat every bite. I devoutly wish all the flight attendants who so obviously hate their jobs, hate their employers, and resent the passengers would have the integrity to quit and go find something else to do. Every time an airline employee lies, his nose should grow. And the hotel industry should be prohibited by an act of Congress from ever using the term "hospitality industry" again. Hospitality my eye.

Anyway, travel is agony for me, which makes me a little obsessive about eking out every ounce of productivity from every trip. Here, I am telling you what I did to survive my peak travel years as well as what I still do when I must pack up and go.

Jam as Much Business into Each Business Trip as Possible

Planning is everything. Once it's determined that I have to go to X city for a particular purpose, then the race is on to find other productive things I can do in that same city or in other cities conveniently located en route. I detest having to get on an airplane, fly somewhere, and come back, all for just one "event."

I think this discipline can extend to everybody. I'm often amazed at how poorly organized territory salespeople are, jumping from one end of their territory to another, back and forth, able to fit in only a few appointments a day when they could double or triple that if determined to do so. I observe service business owners, such as lawn and garden services, pest control services, etc., using shotgun, scattered marketing and winding up with customers here, there, and everywhere. Instead, if they concentrated on dominating a few "tight" geographic areas, they would likely have lots of customers in one place, giving them maximum efficiency in delivering services.

Here's an example of the kind of smart scheduling I like to do: I was booked to speak in Florida on a Thursday, and in the middle of the country the following Tuesday. This allowed me to give a break on expenses to an East Coast consulting client and sell him a day, actually two half-days: Thursday afternoon and Friday morning. I still had time Friday to get to Chicago and get to my favorite harness racing track by its 7:00 P.M. post time and enjoy an evening at the races. Saturday I had lunch with an old friend and a brief, late-afternoon meeting with a prospective client. Sunday was a "dead day"; I stayed in my hotel room and worked on writing projects. Monday, at the airport where I had to change planes, I arranged a two-hour meeting with two business partners, each of whom flew in for the meeting from their homes in two different cities. Monday evening I did a radio talk show interview over the phone, just as I would have if I had been home. None of this happened by accident. Once I had the two "bookend" dates locked in, I very deliberately went to work to fill in the four days in between. My little hierarchical checklist is as follows:

- What can I try to plug in that is directly revenue positive?
- Can I plug in meetings with business partners or courtesy meetings with ongoing, continuing clients or meetings

with my publishers, agents, media contacts, etc., that are indirectly productive?

- Finally, should I plug in any goof-off stuff?

I apply this checklist often. For example, a speaking engagement in Las Vegas forced me to leave my Ohio home. As soon as that commitment took its square on the calendar, I booked a week in a suite at the Paris hotel, then began "fleshing in" the week. I wound up with the speech the morning of the first day, a lunch meeting with a continuing client on that same day, a paid day of consulting the last day (with a client flying there from Los Angeles) and three days of vacation in between—cheated only with a two-hour tele-seminar I hosted from my hotel room. Behind the Vegas week, I wedged in a stop in Phoenix to visit my own office and for a luncheon speaking engagement. On the front side of the trip, I first flew to Denver for a speaking engagement there.

Whether you are leaving your home base to go out into your own city for the day or to distant locales, you ought to work at making the entire foray as valuable as possible.

Where Are those "Friendly Skies," Anyway?

Next, there's the airplane trip itself.

When I first started flying on business, it was civilized. People waited to be called to board, no elbowing, pushing, trampling. At least in first class, the stewardesses—yes, I used *that* word—were actually nice to you. One for every four passengers. Cheerfully helped you find places for your carry-ons. Other passengers behaved themselves. Wore socks with their shoes. Did not fill their space and half of yours with an array of gadgetry that'd make a Radio Shack window display look inadequate. Shut up and read a book. The food was edible, the air was breathable. All a distant memory.

Personally, I always fly first class. I do too much of it, I'm too big of a guy, I'm too easily irritated while traveling to tolerate all the built-in abuse of coach class travel. Still, even as I'm enduring the hardships of first class, I'm still able to be productive doing some work on just about every long flight.

Catch Up on Reading and Snoozing

I find airports and long flights great places to catch up on reading materials that can be discarded afterward. I'll often stuff a pile of catalogs, newsletters, trade journals, and magazines into the outer pouch of my suitcase. I'll leave with a big, fat bulge but return with a thin envelope of torn-out pages or articles, having thrown out 90% of it as I finished reading it. Not only is this a good use of airplane time, but there's a significant psychic satisfaction to lightening your load as you go. I recommend this to anybody who "gets behind" in reading trade and professional journals or similar discardable materials.

Airplane flights are also good for "noodling" a possible solution to a particular problem. The isolation, relative quiet, and freedom from ordinary interruptions provide an environment conducive to thinking. Also, the first-class cabin is a good place to make useful business contacts. But, frankly, I sleep more than half of all the flight time.

Don't Be on the Last Plane Out

From a time management standpoint, you should try never to take the last flight from wherever you're at to wherever you're

going, and you should always have info
alternate, back-up flights. If you trave
aware that the frequency of mechanical
aging of the fleets keeps getting worse,
the record, though, for getting nailed by
years ago, I was on the last America W
I-forget-where, with Ben of Ben & Jer
both enroute to speaking engagements ... ...
That night, America Worst managed not one, not two, but three consecutive "mechanicals" affecting this same flight. Fixed one after an hour, while we were taxiing toward take-off, another, different problem erupted. We went back to the airport and after more delay were taken off the plane. After more delay, they brought a different plane, which, after we had boarded, experienced a mechanical problem! Don't take the last flight!

Making off-peak connections is important; you want to avoid rush hour at Atlanta or O'Hare or actually, anywhere, if you can.

I'm good at avoiding lengthy connections, and I do not find the airline "club rooms" very desirable. But many frequent business travelers use these a lot. Actually, I tend to use the Continental Club in my home city airport pre-departure more than anywhere else.

Consider Alternatives

In the past few years, in part thanks to a post 9-11 boom in demand, "time share" private jet companies have become more competitive, more creative in their pricing options, and an affordable option that a very frequent flyer ought to consider. If I were flying as much today as I did in 1997, 1998, 1999, I would buy into one of these programs without question. In those years,

$70,000.00 on commercial airfare. As near as I can esti-
out three times that amount would have bought enough
e jet hours with NetJets or FlightOptions to do the same
antity of travel. The differential would have been a very good
investment, given the value of each of my hours held hostage in
airports at security checkpoint lines or because of flight delays.

If you fly to cities and rent cars a lot, it's well worth joining and
using Hertz Gold Club or Avis's Preferred Customer program to
bypass lines at the counters and avoid filling out the contract from
scratch each time. If you cab it, consider using pre-arranged sedan
services instead, especially at airports known for long taxi waiting
lines, such as Las Vegas, Newark, or National in Washington, DC.
You can usually have a neatly dressed, courteous, English-
speaking driver waiting for you with a clean, four-door Cadillac
or Lincoln sedan with a car phone. You can instantly be on your
way and spend only an extra $10 to $20 more than cab fare. I'm
amazed at the frequent business travelers I know who are too
cheap to use sedan services, opting instead for standing in line in
the rain and cold to finally go on a thrill ride with Abdul.

Be Kind to Your Body

I can remember, as can some of my road warrior friends,
when zipping back and forth across time zones had no apprecia-
ble effect on me. Not anymore. As you put on some years, travel
takes a greater toll, and you need to schedule time for rest. If I
cross a couple of time zones, I need to allow a little extra time for
rest and recovery. When I was a drinker, I used to have two or
three cocktails and think nothing of it. I don't drink anymore at
all, but friends who drink tell me their metabolism changes have
made drinking booze on flights undesirable. Alcohol has a

heightened effect in the air. On flights I make a point of drinking quite a bit of water, and I often skip the really junky airplane meals or eat only the salad. I hit my 49th birthday while finishing this book, but in "travel years," I'm at least 90. Ignoring the damage done to your body and your psyche by frequent travel is stupid. You need to devise strategies for eating, exercise, rest, and work that mitigate the damage as much as possible.

Nothing's worse—or more damaging to productivity—than getting sick while traveling, or, for that matter, coming down with something immediately on your return home. I am firmly convinced that the risk of catching colds and flu are much, much greater for the frequent traveler, and I think I do a pretty good job keeping my incidences down to two or three a year. The quality of the air in the airplanes has gotten worse (!) since the ban on smoking; the lack of cigarette smoke has allowed the airlines to save money by switching from fresh-air systems to recirculating air systems. The "old" planes had two-thirds fresh air, one-third recirculated; the newest planes use 100% recirculated air, so you are breathing a mixture of all the other passengers' colds, flus, viruses, sweat, etc., roughly every seven to nine minutes. Flight attendant sickness is on the rise, and both employees and passengers are complaining (to no avail). According to the National Academy of Sciences, measured in cubic feet per minute, fresh air circulated inside the average airplane ranges from (best) 150 to the pilots in the cockpit, to 50 to first-class passengers, to 7, to coach passengers. We solved the "secondhand smoke" problem. Now we're getting sick from secondhand air.

This is why you should never aim the overhead air vents directly at your face; contagious germs in that air go into your eyes and—whammo!—you're sick as a dog. I also increase my vitamin intake while traveling and, during prime cold and flu seasons, I megadose vitamin C. There's a relatively new, good product called Airborne, a vitamin-rich and zinc-rich tablet that dissolves in water and makes a fizzy lemon drink. You belt this down immediately before heading for the airport. Pros also advise drinking lots of water during long flights. It seems that dehydration enlarges the tiny, inside-the-nostril pores, which increases your chance of catching infections.

Pack Light

Checking baggage is a giant time-waster, even if your bags don't get lost. I haven't checked baggage more than once or twice in ten years, on thousands of flights. Any male should be able to go for up to two weeks with one large carry-on that fits in the overhead bins plus a briefcase. It's tougher for women, but the smart ones figure out how to do it. (Hint: everything matching one pair of shoes helps.) Otherwise, you must get to the airport earlier every time, you must wait for baggage on arrival—usually 30 minutes or more—and this wait often puts you smack in the middle of a herd waiting in line for cabs or packed like sardines into the rental car company or hotel shuttle bus.

If you are going to one place for multiple days and cannot carry everything you need, FedEx it there ahead of you, and FedEx it back when you leave. It's worth the expense—if your time has any value.

Battling for Productivity in Your Hotel Room

Now you've arrived, you're in your hotel. I've learned to have as many meetings as possible at my hotel, with people coming to me, just as I would if at home in my own office, for the same reason. I can stay in my room working while the other person is arriving. If he's late, I'm still working.

Hotel rooms, of course, are designed by imbeciles. All too often, the only phones are next to the bed and in the bathroom, not on the desk or table. Outlets are all hidden, sometimes as far away from the desk or table as you can get. Feel free to rearrange the room. When I traveled with my laptop computer (which I no longer do), I always packed an extension cord.

If price is not a problem for you, my ranking of hotels with rooms designed well and that, overall, do the best job of serving the business traveler are Westin, Hilton, Marriott, and Hyatt—in that order. Many of these chains have in-room, individual fax machines, which I find very useful. Increasingly, they are bundling electrical outlets, Internet hookups, and the phone conveniently on a desk. The on-airport Hyatt in Orlando, Florida, the Hilton at O'Hare in Chicago, and the Marriott in Detroit, Michigan, are wonderfully convenient.

If price is no object at all, THE best hotels for business travelers are The Four Seasons. There are Four Seasons properties in Austin, Texas; Boston; Chicago; Dallas; Houston; Los Angeles; Maui; New York; Newport Beach, California; Palm Beach, Florida; Philadelphia; San Francisco; Santa Barbara, California; Seattle; Toronto; Vancouver, British Columbia; and Washington, DC. The Vancouver Four Seasons, for example, has in the room a desk, outlet within reach, desk phone, bedside phone AND bathroom phone, and voice mail; plus laundry or dry cleaning pickups and deliveries FOUR times daily; fast room service; overnight shoe shines; and a staff that jumps.

If costs are a big concern, Marriott Courtyards and Fairfield Inns have well-designed rooms where you can spread out, work, and be comfortable, but you sacrifice all sorts of services.

Embassy Suites are good values, and every room is a mini-suite, so you can meet comfortably with as many as three people at a time in the living room half of the suite.

By the way, if you work in your room during the day, you will be tempted to hang the "Please Make Up This Room Early" sign on your door as you leave, to go to a breakfast meeting or such. I know better but still occasionally do it, because it is so easy. However, that sign telegraphs to thieves that the room is unoccupied. It is safer—and more effective—to call "housekeeping," explain that you'll be out only for an hour and ask that the room be made up during that time period. This seems to work about 90% of the time.

Communicating while Traveling

Personally, I refuse to carry a cell phone, but you probably do. It is extremely useful, if you can use it for outbound calling to suit you but not have others using it to reach out and bother you. I watch businesspeople already worn to a frazzle by traveling, piling on the taking or making of cell phone calls while taking every step through the airport, eating, standing in lines, boarding the plane, getting off the plane. They are not doing themselves any favors. If a call is important to make, it deserves a bit more thought and a more conducive environment than the boarding ramp, while you are surrounded by screaming children and being bumped by the cattle drive. Having a cell phone to make different airline reservations or handle problems caused by delays: good. Having it steal all your time: bad.

The routine I've arrived at is to (a) try my best to call into the office once during the day, (b) have faxes waiting for me on arrival at my hotel, and (c) check in at home once each evening. The bigger problem is communicating with clients, returning calls from clients, vendors, etc., and being unable to take return calls. I train my clients, as best they can be trained, to communicate via fax rather than phone, and that pre-empts a lot of telephone tag. I also try to return calls from my hotel, when I can stay in the room for a couple of hours, to take bounceback calls. I will often block two or three hours to sit comfortably in my room and take calls, via pre-arranged, back-to-back phone appointments, and knock them off with maximum efficiency.

Most road warriors now travel with laptops or PDAs, use e-mail, and do much of their distance communication this way. My comment is identical to my advice about the cell phone: if you control and use these tools so they serve you well, fine. Do not let them control you.

If I'm on the road for an extended period of time, big rubber tubs of faxes and mail will be waiting for me on my return. The only way to prevent this daunting mountain from being built is to have all my mail shoved in a big FedEx sack and sent to me once or twice while I'm away. I tend to do this with trips of five days or more. I can get through a few days' mail while watching an in-room movie or Monday Night Football, throw out a lot, jot notes on some, and move some back to the office so action can be taken on it the next morning.

The Extinction of the Travel Agent

In the past few years, the Internet and the airlines have, in unholy alliance, done their level bests to kill off travel agents. The travel agents, by being ignorant of positioning, marketing, and selling successfully against commoditization (they needed my book *No B.S. Sales Success*) stood there and took the beating. Many have closed their doors.

The airlines' behavior has been reprehensible. By slashing commissions, blocking agents from assisting clients with mileage redemptions, and aggressively switching customers to Web sites and direct, online purchasing, they have engaged in a very deliberate industry conspiracy to destroy the travel agents.

For frequent business travelers, profound dangers abound in buying air travel direct, online, or through secretarial staff. In a procedure exposed in several national TV news programs but still mostly unknown to travelers, discount tickets purchased online and tickets purchased from independent, nonairline Web sites often carry "secret codes" that move these passengers to the very bottom of the pecking order whenever anything goes wrong. Many of these tickets and Web site ticket sellers have truly bizarre "weasel clauses" and fine print warnings and restrictions. I have several clients who have shared true horror stories with me about being stranded for several days with these tickets. Conversely, I'm amused by people I know willing to spend 30 or 60 minutes or more searching the Internet for fare discounts. I am certainly not willing to trade away a $1,000.00 hour of my time for $87.00 in discounts.

I find a competent travel agent worth his weight in gold. I use the agent to check different flights, fax me options, check every possible connection and cost, maximize my frequent flyer miles, and think for me so I don't always have to remember to ask the right hotel questions, to arrange for a limo, and so forth. An agent like this saves untold amounts of time in planning, and on the trips themselves.

As You Head Out the Door . . .

Road trip! As you head to the airport or the highway, you have to ask yourself if you have a real strategy for maximum efficiency and productivity; minimum stress and agony. There's nothing that can ruin a schedule, suck up more time, sap more energy, and otherwise cause more chaos and problems than travel, so you must take many proactive steps to protect yourself—and your time—as best you can.

CHAPTER 9

How to Handle
the Information
Avalanche

I had a great idea this morning, but I didn't like it.

—SAM GOLDWYN

*S*upposedly, we are in the Paperless Age. But, according to University Microfilms, we're now creating *one billion pages* of information each and every day here in the United States alone. Sometimes I think most of it crosses *my* desk!

People are struggling to cope with the avalanche of information. I get as big an avalanche as anybody. Here's what goes on, for me. First of all, I have all the trade and professional journals, new books, association newsletters, and other documents related to my three primary businesses—direct marketing, infomercial production, and speaking—to keep up with. I have all the general business press to be concerned with, from *Entrepreneur* and *Inc.*

to *Forbes, Fortune,* and *The Wall Street Journal.* As a consultant, I'm often "learning" several new businesses in connection with my clients, so I read their trade publications, too. Because of the infomercial business, I watch a lot of television, and I review about 20 hours of videotape every month. Because I do so much work with direct-mail, I read ALL of my "junk mail." And I read at least one book a week. Fortunately, I speed read. But, still . . . .

How Do You Handle All This?

I'm sure you are digging out from under your own avalanche of information everyday, too. Let me offer you some "shovels."

IMPROVE YOUR READING SKILLS

Many people are poor readers and insist that they do not "like" to read. Sadly, our U.S. universities and high schools alike are churning out mass numbers of young people who do not read, get all their news from TV or radio, and, in a shocking number of cases, are borderline illiterate. Once again, honesty with yourself is the best policy. Hire a tutor if necessary. If not, then take or get a good home study speed reading course. Speed reading (and speed comprehension) is real.

By the way, I think you MUST read, as you can see in the accompanying article (Figure 9.1), that I originally wrote for one of my newsletters.

GET ONLY THE INFORMATION YOU REALLY WANT AND NEED

If you are really busy, and time is much more of an issue than money, you can pay others to read for you. There are "clipping services," including one run by *The Wall Street Journal,* that will

FIGURE **9.1**

APPARENTLY, YOU ARE NOW AN AMAZING ODDITY AKIN TO A THREE-HEADED COW—IF YOU READ. The Saturday after Christmas, working in my office, I had the weekend *Today Show* on the TV, and jerked my head around to watch when I heard this amazing statement, delivered with breathless excitement:

> *"Coming up next—we'll interview the woman who read a book a week for a year and has written her own book about the experience!"*

What!?! With brief lapses here and there, I've read at least a book a week every year for more than 30 years. What's the big deal about this? Well, apparently it is a big deal. The last time I went to Barnes & Noble, I bought a new biography of Ben Franklin, Tom Peters' new book, a couple of other business books, a book about stroke-free living, three paperback novels to take on airplanes, and about 20 magazines. The clerk said: "Lifetime's supply, huh?" Sheesh.

You MUST read a lot to succeed. Here are the reasons: (1) Varied, diverse input, ideas, viewpoints, life stories, examples, all the essential raw material poured into your subconscious mind, for it to sift, sort, try matching up with other puzzle pieces it already has, so it can occasionally yell "Eureka!" and hand you something profitable—without daily flow of new stuff, it just sleeps. Wealth secret: you cannot manufacture anything without raw material. Not even

---

FIGURE **9.1**, continued

money. (2) Without exposure to others' thinking, your own range of thought shrinks. Soon, you're a mental midget. Your range of thought narrows, like your range of motion shrinks if you don't move and stretch. (3) You can't stay current. I read a monstrous amount and I still can't stay current. If you're not reading a book or two, a dozen magazines, a few newspapers, and a few newsletters every week, you must be way, way, way behind. Pretty soon, your conversation reveals you as a dinosaur. (4) If you have kids, you want to set a decent example for them. They need to see you reading. They need to hear you talking about what you read. When I was a kid, the years my family was dead broke, we made a regularly scheduled, weekly treks to the public library for an hour or so. My father, mother, and I each picked out three or four books for the week, took them home, read them, and talked about them. Now I prefer going to the bookstore, because I have money, and like keeping the books. However, I'm grateful for the library-habit years. It would be a better thing for most families to do than going to the movies, arcade, or Wal-Mart.

Historical note I had in a book I wrote back in 1985: the town leaders of Franklin, Massachusetts, once wrote and asked Ben Franklin for a donation so they could buy a bell for the church steeple. He sent money with this note: "I'm honored you have named your town Franklin and a donation is enclosed. However, I suggest you start a library with it rather than buying a bell. I prefer sense to sound."

ferret through hundreds of daily newspapers, trade magazines, etc., for the topic you have requested and fax to you just the articles about your topic. You may have a staff person read and clip for you. A good project for son, daughter, grandson, granddaughter is a regular pile of reading, like trade journals, to clip, highlight, even summarize for you. One of my clients pays his high-school-age son $75.00 a week to read 14 different trade journals and newsletters and record summaries and excerpts on a weekly tape that he can listen to while he drives to work.

Set Aside and "Bulk" Material that Is Not Time Sensitive, to Review at Your Leisure

Catalogs, interesting-looking junk mail, and popular magazines fall into this category. You MUST be very selective about what warrants your attention now, what later, what never.

Consider Condensation

You can subscribe to *Executive Book Summaries,* for example, and get brief summaries of a dozen new, "hot" business books every month. This is sort of a Cliff Notes for adults. There's a similar service, *Newstrack,* for news buffs.

Use Your VCR, DVD, or TIVO

Tape programs of interest or importance to you, then watch them at your convenience.

Use Your "Drive Time" or Travel Time as Learning Time

Here are the average to-and-from-the-office commute times for major cities: New York, 1 hour, 5 minutes; Washington DC, 1 hour;

Houston, 1 hour; L.A., 1 hour, 30 minutes; Dallas, 48 minutes; Phoenix, 46 minutes; Buffalo, 40 minutes. Because most audio-cassettes are about 40 minutes in length, you can finish a cassette a day. Half a cassette (one side) per drive. And these days, every-thing is available on audiocassette: people like me; experts in various fields. Tapes on business, finance, health, sex, self-improvement, foreign languages, travel, lectures from great col-lege professors'; classic and contemporary fiction; you name it. If you average 40 minutes a day x 250 workdays, that's 167 "class-room hours" a year available to you.

Resist the Siren Song of Distraction
A lot of people let "noninformation" consume a lot of their time. Today's news is tomorrow's fish-wrap, yet we have just about become consumed with useless news. Twenty-four-hour-a-day news stations; *60 Minutes* beget *60 Minutes II; 20/20, 20/20 Downtown; Dateline* twice a week. News-talk radio. Etc. Yes, you want to be informed. But do you need to be informed about the latest celebrity sex or shoplifting scandal, the latest athlete going to jail, the weather in Bulgaria?

Use Technology, but Resist Seduction by Technology
Technology is terrific when it *really* enhances productivity. But all too often it only gives the illusion of that. People who spend hours on end roaming the Internet or in e-mail dialogue don't fool me. This is just another escape into busyness, just like going to one darned meeting after another.

However, virtually every newspaper is now online, so if you are traveling to a distant city and would benefit from being familiar with that city's current news, it's readily available.

Most associations and trade journals have useful archives. My Gold, Gold+, and Gold/VIP Members have access to a members'-only section of my dankennedy.com site, with transcripts of past interviews with experts, articles, past newsletters, and other reference material.

Specialize. But Not too Much.

It is probably better to know a great deal about one, two, or several things than a tiny bit about everything. Specialization almost always adds value. And it can be used to limit information flow.

In business, I specialize in direct-response advertising and direct-mail, with a subspecialty in "long form" (copy intensive) advertising, and another subspecialty in the marketing of information products. As a result, I rarely bother reading *Advertising Age* magazine, a trade journal for traditional advertising professionals, but I do read *Direct Marketing* magazine and *DIRECT*. Being able NOT to read something is very useful.

However, too narrow of focus becomes myopia. If you exclude too much information and input, you rob your brain of the raw material needed for breakthrough ideas. Most people in a particular industry are so myopic they start committing what I call "marketing incest"—with the same result as real incest; after just a few generations, everybody's stupid. People in "x" business look at what everybody else in "x" business is doing, they go to association meetings together, read the same trade journals, and copy from each other. Getting outside this box is important.

So, you need a balance. A lot of specialization, but not too much specialization.

Know What You Are Looking For

Dealing with today's overwhelming quantity of information is a bit like looking for the proverbial needle in a haystack. That task is made less daunting because you know you are looking for a needle. It would be even worse if you were just told to go through the entire hay mound and look for *something*.

So, here's a little test (Figure 9.2) I give to my clients that you might try taking at the end of each week. It will help you focus, help you spot the right things, and find the needles in the haystack of the week ahead.

FIGURE **9.2**

What Do You Know This Week, That You Didn't Know Last Week, About . . .

1. Your business? _____

   _____

2. Your industry as a whole? _____

   _____

3. Your competitors? _____

   _____

4. Your customers or clients as a group? _____

   _____

5. Your top 10, 20, or 30 customers or clients? _____

   _____

6. A client, individually? _____

   _____

7. One of the top leaders in your field? _____

   _____

8. Societal, cultural, or economic trends that may affect your
   business? _____

   _____

9. A "success" topic—personal finance, self-motivation, time
   management? _____

   _____

10. A "marketing" topic—direct-response advertising, construction
    of offers, copy that sells, direct mail, the Internet? _____

    _____

11. A person, event, or topic in the current news of great interest
    or importance to your clientele? _____

    _____

12. A "method"—a means, process, technique of doing something
    useful to you, whether manufacturing your widget faster or
    making a sales presentation more effectively? _____

    _____

If you actually discipline yourself to get one answer to each question worth putting down in writing just once a week, after a year, you'll be 624 big steps ahead of your peers and competitors. And the odds are excellent you'll have uncovered a few ultra-valuable gems. Keeping these questions in the forefront of your mind is a way of "electrifying and magnetizing your antenna," so casual conversations or even an overheard conversation can yield something useful you'd otherwise never have noticed.

How to Organize and Manage Ideas

The great success educator Earl Nightingale wrote that "a single thought can revolutionize your life. A single thought can make you rich or well-to-do, or it can land you in prison for the rest of your life. Everything was an idea before it became real in the world . . . the law of averages begins to swing in your direction when you begin to produce ideas."

"Ideas," Earl said, "are like slippery fish."

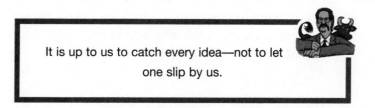

It is up to us to catch every idea—not to let one slip by us.

For many years, I used a strategy adapted from Michael Vance, a close associate of Walt Disney, called the storyboard. I had a corked wall in my office, with vertical columns, each column headed by a business or project title. Then, every time I had an idea, I'd jot it down on a small card, about half of a 3 x 5-inch card, and pushpin it up there in the correct column. I carried a little supply of cards with me at all times, so I never lost an idea. Frankly, for a while, I drifted away from that; now I've returned.

I also maintain different "project notebooks" or even legal pads dedicated to one project.

I have a pad and pen everywhere. Even in the bathroom.

Some people are very adept at verbalizing their ideas, so they carry micro-recorders, dictate, have a staff person or service transcribe it all, then organize it. My brain engages with pen in hand or fingers on keyboard.

The important thing is for you to choose and use *some* method for capturing every idea that comes to you, wherever, and whenever it happens.

Bulk is a problem for many of us. My friend Lee Milteer has research, reference, and project piles in gigantic clear plastic bags, so she can see what's in them. My piles have 4 x 6-inch title cards on them. I have more than 1,000 books on shelves, but if I read a book with only a few worthwhile pages, I tear out the pages, file them, then throw out the book. The computer with the CD-ROM is obviously a major tool in reducing bulk for information storage. From a time standpoint, the trick is to be able to quickly find what you need when you need it—my own Achilles heel.

How the Well-Trained, Conditioned, and Fit Subconscious Mind Helps Handle the Information Avalanche

From the mid-1950s to 1960, Dr. Maxwell Maltz worked devising and perfecting practical methods for making the subconscious mind fitter and more useful. His work is summarized in his classic best-selling book *Psycho-Cybernetics* and in the recently updated companion I co-authored, *The New Psycho-Cybernetics*. Dr. Maltz's findings and methods have been of enormous importance to me my entire life, and I urge you to investigate them for yourself. Specific to being more productive, and to better managing and utilizing information, you can deliberately make your subconscious work better as a finder, organizer, and provider of whatever you need to make a presentation, write a sales letter, whatever. This is beyond ordinary memory. This is a *creative* retrieval process.

For example, I, like most direct-response ad copywriters, maintain a room full of what we call "swipe files." These are files of samples by category. One file contains "Headlines, Weight Loss Ads," another "Headlines, Income Opportunity Ads." There are files for opening sentences, guarantees, offers, and on and on. Hundreds and hundreds and hundreds of them. Huge notebooks. Reference books. It takes a lot of time to go through all the relevant ones physically, in preparing to write copy for a client. Sometimes that's unavoidable, but quite often, for me, it is

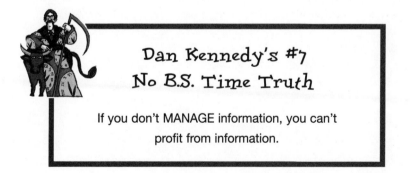

Dan Kennedy's #7 No B.S. Time Truth

If you don't MANAGE information, you can't profit from information.

not. Instead, I give my subconscious mind the assignment of going through its stored "swipe files" to find the right idea, "hook," or starting point for a particular ad—*while I sleep* ! When I wake, the idea spews out through my fingers onto my computer screen. This is not a happy accident or some freakish mind mutation unique to me. It is the result of deliberate training with Psycho-Cybernetics. It probably liberates me from at least 20 hours of hard labor every month.

CHAPTER 10

Fire Yourself, Replace Yourself, Make More Money, and Have More Fun

You all look like happy campers to me. Happy campers you are, happy campers you have been and, as far as I'm concerned, happy campers you will always be.

—VICE-PRESIDENT DAN QUAYLE, ADDRESSING A GROUP OF SAMOANS

There are all sorts of things that make entrepreneurs unhappy. We detest government interference, government red tape, and government stupidity. Vendors who fail to keep commitments or meet quality standards make us unhappy. Bankers and lawyers bring us much unhappiness. (Risky these days to joke about terrorists, but maybe you heard of the terrorists who hijacked a plane full of lawyers returning from a convention. The terrorists warned that, if their demands were not met, they'd release ten lawyers every hour.) But, above all else, the thing that makes entrepreneurs most miserable—although they may not easily recognize it—is *routine.*

Entrepreneurs make lousy managers and administrators because too much of that work is routine.

This tells you a lot about what you must do in order to achieve maximum success, derive maximum value from your time, and lead the happiest possible life: you must systematically, aggressively divest yourself of those activities you do not do well, do not do happily, or find routine, so as to systematically invest your time (and talent, knowledge, know-how, and other resources) in those things you do extraordinarily well, enjoy doing, and find intellectually stimulating.

I have just described for you a formula for peak personal productivity, as a specialist. And you ought to note that, in every field of enterprise, specialists outearn generalists ten to one. Heart surgeons vs. M.D.s. Sophisticated database computer program developers vs. programmers. Nuclear waste disposal experts vs. garbage men. And so on.

But having said that, how do we make that happen? How do we get there? It certainly is easier said than done. But you can start moving in this direction today, step by step, just as I have.

"We're Overpaying Him, but He's Worth It"

The movie magnate Samuel Goldwyn, famous for butchering the language, said that. Actually, your business is overpaying you for some of the jobs you do and grossly underpaying you for others.

Step One: Honest Self-Analysis and Self-Understanding

The typical entrepreneur—myself included—believes, no, *knows*, absolutely knows that he can do anything and everything, because, at some point in time, we have had to. However, even though I can do it all, truth is, there are only a few things I do so extraordinarily well that—even if given all the money in the world—I wouldn't hire anybody else to do them. There are only a few things I do better than anybody else on the planet. Truth be told, you have only a few things in that category too. Then, you and I have another couple of handfuls of things we do well, better than most, but cannot be considered our "specialties." And there are any number of things you and I do that we do out of necessity, don't do very well, but do them anyway.

If you're honest with yourself, you can create these three lists. (And it's a very productive exercise to sit down alone and make these three lists.)

"Delegate or Stagnate"
Step Two: Delegation

Of course, delegating is as hard for entrepreneurs as telling the truth is for politicians. It's downright unnatural. Why? Habit, for one thing. We create our businesses from scratch, do it all, develop a way of doing things that we believe in, and find that habit is hard to break. No one is ever going to do things exactly the same way we do them.

Jay Van Andel, co-founder of the giant Amway Corporation impressed me many years ago with a speech titled, "Delegate or Stagnate." Of course, the entire Amway system is based on multiplication of effort; one person learning a set of skills, then duplicating himself over and over again. And Jay and his partner, Rich DeVos, had a business that grew like topsy. In order to stay ahead of it, they constantly delegated and—ultimately—replaced themselves over and over again, which we'll get to in a minute. What

Jay made very clear to me is that the only way to advance in any business is to keep delegating.

THERE'S MORE THAN ONE WAY TO BE RIGHT

Brendan Suhr, the assistant head coach of the Detroit Pistons during their championship years in the 1980s, said to me: "Do you know how many head coaches there are in the NBA? Well, there are at least that many different ways to be right, because every one of these coaches does things differently, yet they all represent the top ⅒% of the coaching profession. There are 1,000 guys who'd like every one of these jobs. There are at least 100 guys who'd be good candidates for every one of these jobs. So these head coaches all do it "right," yet they all do it differently." His point is valid.

You cannot delegate if you believe there's only one way to get things done right.

OFTEN, GOOD ENOUGH IS GOOD ENOUGH

Let me give you an example: I used to have a business associate, a key person in my company, a $100,000.00 a year guy—whose time had to be worth more than $250.00 an hour. It so happened he had a fetish about how boxes were packed. When we were leaving for a week-long series of seminars, instead of attending to any number of important responsibilities, he'd be back in the shipping department for hours, doing the job of the $10.00 an hour shipping clerk. I've got to admit that he packed a wicked box. I mean, this guy's boxes were works of art. They were very, very carefully packed, firm to the top and the corners, so that no corner crumpled in. The tape was perfectly straight. The bottom and sides were taped just as perfectly as the top. Every label was

Dan Kennedy's #8
No B.S. Time Truth

Good enough is good enough.

on straight. However, in the many years since he has been gone, our shipping clerks shipped thousands of cartons to my seminar sites. Not packed quite as well. Corners crumpled a little bit now and again. Tape crooked. Labels cockeyed. But every one of these boxes got there. The product was fine. The result was the same. Good enough is good enough.

Many, many things can be delegated to people who will not do them the way you would, won't do them as perfectly as you would, but will wind up with the same result. Every one of these things should be delegated. In fact, you MUST delegate. You cannot move ahead without jettisoning some responsibilities and tasks in order to make room for new, more valuable tasks and responsibilities.

And I'm not necessarily talking about creating a giant managerial bureaucracy. Today, you can delegate to independent contractors, freelancers, and vendors, too. Outsourcing is the buzzword of the day, with good reason. Also, if you have anybody around you with intelligence and talent, you must keep giving them new, more important responsibilities and getting them to delegate.

Mastering Delegation

You MUST master this difficult skill. To delegate effectively, here's the seven-step process.

1. Define what is to be done.
2. Be certain the delegatee understands what is to be done.
3. Explain why it is to be done as you are prescribing it to be done.
4. Teach how it is to be done without micro-micro-managing.
5. Be sure the delegatee understands the how-to process.
6. Set the deadline for completion or progress report.
7. Be sure you have agreement to the date or time and method.

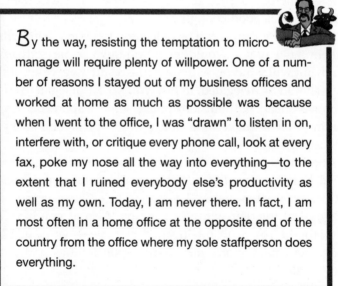

By the way, resisting the temptation to micro-manage will require plenty of willpower. One of a number of reasons I stayed out of my business offices and worked at home as much as possible was because when I went to the office, I was "drawn" to listen in on, interfere with, or critique every phone call, look at every fax, poke my nose all the way into everything—to the extent that I ruined everybody else's productivity as well as my own. Today, I am never there. In fact, I am most often in a home office at the opposite end of the country from the office where my sole staffperson does everything.

This is not rocket science. But it takes very deliberate patience. It even takes time. But investing time in getting good at this and getting people around you who respond to it is the only way to get time freed up to do more valuable things yourself.

Going Beyond Delegation

And, as difficult as all this is, it's just the beginning. The real, big, blockbuster secret of entrepreneurial success and happiness goes beyond delegation to replacement.

Step Three: Replacing Yourself

My Platinum Member Rory Fatt, president of Restaurant Marketing Systems, exhorts the thousands of restaurant owners he advises: "Fire yourself! You'll make more money and have more fun." The disease exists in every industry, but Rory says it's epidemic and endemic in restaurants—owners terminally inflicted with the belief that they must be the one making the sauce, greeting the guests at the door, doing the inventory. They are so busy doing the $10.00-an-hour jobs, they never get to do the $100.00-an-hour job: marketing to bring in new customers, and to keep customers coming back. Rory says you can hire just about anybody to wash glasses, and there are a lot of people you can hire to make the sauce, but there's hardly anybody you can hire to effectively market and promote the restaurant.

"They Gave Me a Lifetime Contract, Then They Pronounced Me Legally Dead"

I agree with Rory—most business owners need to fire themselves from a lot of those $10.00-an-hour jobs. The late college basketball coach Jim Valvano wrote a book long before his death from cancer with the above title as a sardonic poke at his field. It's said there are only three kinds of coaches: those just getting hired, those just fired, and those soon to be fired. Jimmy Johnson took the Dallas Cowboys to two Super Bowls in a row, then was fired. Nobody, and I mean nobody is indispensable. The day Johnny Carson retired, the entire country wondered if the *Tonight Show* would soon die. So did NBC. But we have become loyal to Jay Leno, and a whole lot of people might not recognize Johnny Carson if they bumped into him on the street. Jack Paar couldn't even get onto the studio property without an ID card.

Step Four: Welcoming Your Dispensability

Most people do not like the idea of dispensability. The entrepreneur on vacation is schizophrenic: hoping everything's OK at the office but disappointed when he calls in and finds out everything *is* OK at the office. How can things be running smoothly without him? I'm going to try and sell you on welcoming your own dispensability.

Entrepreneurs grow in experience and expertise very quickly. Fast learners. You will probably master entire "chunks" of a business in a matter of months, yet you may continue doing those same functions for years. This will lead to stagnation and unhappiness. You may even wind up ineffectively doing things you could do well just out of boredom. The ultimate answer is replacement. That is, you replace yourself and step up to a new set of opportunities and responsibilities. You groom someone to take your place.

Note that this is the opposite of executive behavior in a corporate bureaucracy. In that environment, the executive is desperately afraid of the up-and-comers who would take over his job. The executive is determined to protect his turf. Through secrecy, deliberate confusion, corporate politics, and every other imaginable method, the executive tries to make himself indispensable. The super-savvy entrepreneur does the opposite and tries to make himself dispensable.

I have gone through many different scenarios in my business life. I had 42 employees; then for quite a while five; now only one. I have delegated a lot, I've delegated almost nothing, and done everything myself. I confess I am still guilty of doing some menial tasks myself rather than supervise anyone. Beginning in 1999, I aggressively switched from delegation to replacement of a sort. I sold my information products business then. In 2003, I sold my newsletter business. I've arrived at what I call my "Dan as Center of Universe Strategy": me in the middle and satellite businesses owned and managed by others all based on me, my writings, my other content, all paying me. Right now, there are four such satellites.

A good question to consider is, what plan you are working on to reduce your business' and income's dependency on your own time and effort?

What to Do with the Time You Liberate

One thing you can do is enjoy the success you create. Golf, buy racehorses and hang out at the track (a passion of mine), write, get involved in community service or politics, whatever.

If you're looking for the answer that turns your time into the most money and wealth possible, then turn your attention to marketing. Get free of as many other aspects of your business as

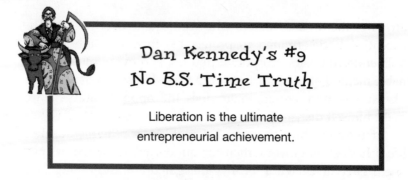

Dan Kennedy's #9
No B.S. Time Truth

Liberation is the ultimate
entrepreneurial achievement.

you can, get passionately interested in and good at marketing, and invest your time there. Why? Because it is infinitely easier to find or train someone to take care of a business' operations than it is to get someone to do its marketing. Marketing is the highest-paid profession and most valuable part of a business. The person who can create systems for acquiring customers, clients, or patients effectively and profitably is the "money person." He is the equivalent of a "high impact" or "franchise" player in sports.

Let me give you a quick example: a big publisher of a variety of different newsletters, on average, hires and pays only four or five professional copywriters each year to write the sales letters that acquire new subscribers for those newsletters. The copy-writer who can create a successful sales letter for this company will rarely be paid less than $250,000.00 in a year, in fees and roy-alties—for writing just one letter! Find me any other kind of writer who can command $250,000.00 for eight pages. You can't find a novelist. A screenwriter. A technical writer. A journalist. No one gets $250,000.00 for eight pages.

In my book *Make Millions with Your Ideas* (Plume/Dutton), I tell the story of the turnaround of the now-famous Thighmaster from a terribly unsuccessful product to a huge, megamillions of dollars success. The person who figured out the three "little" things to do to "fix" that product's marketing (described in my book) received millions of dollars.

Now I have what should be very exciting news: most of the top-flight, most successful marketing wizards are entrepreneurs who grew up into marketers, and who are self-taught, many in very short periods of time. What they have done to become what they are—people whose time is worth thousands of dollars per hour—you can do too. Yes, I am here to tell you that you can, over a two-to-five year term, make your hours each worth $1,000.00 or more.

Join me. Free yourself from boring routine and modest pay-off activity and graduate to life as a "Master Marketer."

CHAPTER 11

A Baker's Dozen
of Productivity-Builder
Tips and Ideas

It's been 24 hours since I last heard from my creditors,
and yet, it seems like only yesterday.

—GEORGE MARENTIS IN QUOTE MAGAZINE

*S*ome things just don't warrant a whole chapter to say. It'd be a crime in a book about productivity enhancement to waste time "padding" such a thing up to a full chapter, don't you think?

Lie Down with Dogs; Wake Up with Fleas

It's not really me that's late; it's the others who are always in a hurry.

—MARILYN MONROE

Yes, who you hang out with matters. Who you employ definitely matters. No matter how strong you think your character is, you cannot help but be influenced by the people you are around most of the time. This is why imprisoning first-time offenders with hardened, repeat criminals only serves to graduate more determined, vicious criminals. "Association" is one of the most powerful forces on the face of the earth. Ignore it at your peril.

So, if you insist on hanging around people with nominal integrity, you will soon find yourself lying, cheating, conning, stealing, and abusing with greater and greater ease, less and less guilt. Hanging around poor people is no way to grow rich. And if you hang around people who place very little value on time—theirs, others', or passing time in general—your own productivity will diminish.

Any tennis player, golfer, or other athlete will tell you: if you really want to improve your game, practice and play with people a notch or two better at it than you are.

That's why it's best to associate yourself with busy, productive, effective, successful people. And to eradicate the real time wasters from your life.

Mañana

I am a believer in punctuality although it makes me very lonely.

—Edward Verral Lucas

When you go to Mexico—or for that matter, Nassau, a favorite of mine—you have to take off your watch and force yourself into slow motion, because these people have absolutely no sense of urgency whatsoever. And nothing you might do will alter that. If you can't put yourself into that mode and enjoy it, stay away. You might hurt somebody.

Of course, that's fine on vacation. But it is very frustrating for me to deal with so many people *in business* who have so little urgency. Most people do take the attitude that whatever we don't get done today, we'll get to tomorrow, and what's the big deal?

Instilling a continuing, constant sense of urgency in others is extremely difficult. A few get it. Most don't. This is one of a collection of reasons that, contrary to all of government's ill-fated, Robin Hoodesque efforts, 5% of the people get 95% of the money. We have a sense of urgency the 95%ers don't.

If it really matters to you whether a letter gets out today or tomorrow, whether a mailing makes it out on Friday so it moves over the weekend or waits until Monday, or whether a project gets finished as promised, then you automatically get more done than just about everybody else because those things matter little to them.

Most folks work slow. Watch 'em. There is an old time management axiom: work expands to fill the time available to do it. For most people work expands, period. And very few people ever complete a project before time runs out and come looking for something else to do. In my operation, when my mother left the office, it would have taken three "regular" employees to replace her if my wife hadn't stepped in. But most people work slow. I watch them with amazement. Make a phone call, take a break.

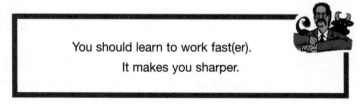

You should learn to work fast(er).
It makes you sharper.

I like to put myself under the time-gun to get things done. Maybe I learned this as a kid, in the barns at the racetrack. If you're a caretaker, when the trainer takes your horse out for his morning workout, you've got about 15 minutes or a bit less to get that horse's stall mucked and bedded down with fresh straw, the feed bucket cleaned, fresh water in the water bucket, and the next horse harnessed and ready to go before the trainer returns. It takes about 13 minutes to do all that if you work fast and non-stop. That's a time-gun. In many cases today, I know in my head how much time it should take me to do a certain project, and that's all the time I allot for it.

How to Use the Home Office to Increase Personal Productivity

You can't have everything. Where would you put it?

—COMEDIAN STEVEN WRIGHT

My client, friend, and, most recently, joint venture partner Jeff Paul wrote a marvelous little book, *How to Make $4,000.00 a Day, Sitting at Home, in Your Underwear*. More than 300,000 copies have been sold. The book is actually about how to succeed in the mail-order business, but it turns out that the title has struck a chord with hundreds of thousands of people. Response, when the book was advertised in national magazines, was incredible. Why? Because people have just about had it with one-to-two-hour com-mutes, bumper to bumper, inch by inch, surrounded by toxic exhaust fumes.

There are now an estimated 65 million people working from home, some full-time, some part-time. And that number keeps increasing, thanks to evolving employer flexibility, entrepreneur-ial growth, new and improved technology, and worsening com-mutes. Those of us in marketing have coined the name "SoHo

Market" to describe the small or "micro" business and home-operated business explosion. Most new home builders are putting home office rooms in the model homes.

Back when I wrote the first edition of this book, *Home Office Computing* magazine's surveys indicated that 96% to 98% of the people working from home were happier than they were working at an off-site store or office, and would recommend it as a lifestyle to others. I hear both viewpoints from my clients. Some find they cannot work at home, mostly because of their own inability to avoid readily available distractions. Most, however, prefer it, and believe they are more productive. A telecommuting consultant quoted in Paul and Sarah Edwards' book *Working from Home* insists that measured productivity increases by 15% to 25% when working from home.

I can be from bed and bath to productivity in five minutes. If you have a 45-minute commute, that 90-minute daily round trip takes nine work weeks of possible productivity right out of your calendar. On January 1, you can cross off two months plus a week. Making this up, just to get back to even, takes a multiple of that. Not to mention the attitudinal impact of a smelly, grungy, aggravating, and often hazardous, daily commute.

When I am able to spend the entire day working at home, I do not take off for an hour or hour and a half to go to lunch; I walk over to the kitchen, make myself lunch, (eat healthier more often than not), and happily munch while I mush on. I get to make telephone calls while sitting in my massager-recliner, having a back massage, or out on my deck. There are few, if any, interruptions, so I gain momentum, and get more done. So much more that I can take an hour-or-so afternoon nap and still be way ahead of what I would have accomplished in a conventional office environment. Why wouldn't you want to work this way?

Yes, there are trade-offs. Office invariably expands from its confined, single room to other places in the house. Maybe the business is more on your mind (I'm not sure). To me, it's a trade worth making.

Different people find different settings lead to their best productivity. Thoreau had to go off and sit by a pond, away from everybody else, to be productive. If that's what you find you have to do, grab some mosquito repellent, hook up a cell phone and fax in your car if you want, pack a lunch, and head off into the sunrise. My friend Jeff Paul cannot stand the sight of a necktie and is at his best in old, grubby sweats, at home. Fine. Some people need the socialization of being in an office or office building with other people. If that's you, then the whole idea of working from home may be wrong although there are ways to inject socialization: taking a coffee break and calling a friend, for example. You ought to experiment a bit, figure out what works best for you, and do that.

How to Drown in Opportunity and Success

Just say "No."

—Nancy Reagan

Most entrepreneurs go through long periods of struggle and suffering before achieving what often looks to the outside observer like "overnight success." I spent years laboring in oblivion, even ignominy. I have had cars repossessed, been hounded by creditors, gone bankrupt, been so broke that I've had to scrounge change from under the couch cushions to get something to eat, driven old "beater" cars. I have been ridiculed, ignored, and abused. I have had enough of all this to be very, very appreciative of opportunity and good fortune. And to worry that it could all dry up tomorrow morning, too. In some respects, this paranoia is healthy. I have seen the opposite many times: the person on a roll who starts buying into his own PR, believing it will never end, spending like a drunken sailor, piling up overhead, and treating people arrogantly. Then it does dry up. The crash is brutal.

On the other hand, this paranoia makes it difficult to say "no." Yet, the biggest single job of the time-conscious, productivity-oriented entrepreneur is saying no.

Saying "no" to opportunity is painful. But necessary. Because the more successful you get, the more opportunities flow your way. People line up. But if you say "yes" to everybody and everything, you will soon drown in your own success.

Determining what *not* to do today is also important. There will always be more things to do than time available to do them. More calls to make, more people to talk to, more places to go, more details to check up on than there is time available to do them. And this doesn't diminish with success; it becomes more so.

For the person eager to do things right, who aspires to "excellence," it is emotionally difficult to leave things undone, to know that there are things that should have been attended to that weren't. But you have to make that adjustment or age rapidly before your time. You can only do what you can do; you cannot do anymore. There's never a day that goes by without a phone call or two I would like to have returned that are never made, letters I would like to have written that are undone, projects I'd love to have completed that are never even looked at. All I can do every day is start out with a plan, a list of priorities, make as few reactive adjustments as possible during the day, and deal first with the life-or-death priorities, and then on down the list. Have a powerful sense of urgency and do all that you can do, but then, when the clock runs out on your workday, relax.

When you make your "to-do lists," by the way, it's important not to hopelessly overload the list. The tendency to pile on more than can be done is understandable. I catch myself taking more work with me on a road trip than I could possibly handle in three trips. It's the same thing. But done consistently, it becomes depressing. It decreases productivity. Again, deciding what *not* to do is very important.

Short-Term, Medium-Term, and Long-Term Thinking

If you don't know where you are going,
you might end up somewhere else.

—YOGI BERRA

Early in my speaking career, a speaker and friend of mine, Keith DeGreen suggested that a speaker should have a short-term market, where you work a lot early, to get experience, make money, and pay the bills; a medium-term market, where you want to become known and successful over a two-to-five-year term; and a long-term market, where you want to sustain a career over 5 to 15 years. And you must devote some time to all 3 at once.

I used this idea specific to speaking, but I also apply it on a broader basis. In fact, I think every entrepreneur ought to use it. Right now, your short-term thinking has to be applied to the exact business you're in today, as it is today: what can we do to increase sales, attract new customers, better retain and do more business with past customers, boost profits, solve management problems, improve employees' performance, improve vendor responsiveness, find capital?

But, at the same time, you must devote some time to medium-term thinking: what do I want this business to be like two years, three years, four years from now? What changes are happening in my industry, in my community, with my customers that I must keep pace with? The great speaker, the late Ira Hayes, called this kind of thinking "keeping pace with tomorrow."

And, at the same time, you should devote some time to long-term thinking, integrating business with lifestyle: what do you want your life to be like five to ten years down the road? I think you need to be investing some time (and some money) in long-term plays, designed to start yielding benefits years down the road.

Get Rid of Nuisances

*Nothing is so fatiguing as the eternal nagging
on of an uncompleted task.*

—WILLIAM JAMES

From time to time, a "chore" will land in your lap that is repugnant. It may be an accounting matter, a problem employee, a government report, whatever. You'll catch yourself taking this off the top of the pile, moving it to the bottom of the pile, over and over again. Don't. The best thing to do with such a nuisance is do it and get rid of it as quickly as possible. It ain't wine; it won't get better with age. The longer you let one of these things hang around, the more reluctance to deal with it you build up.

By the way, the best management advice I ever got was: hire slow, fire fast. If you've got a problem employee hanging around, you know it, he knows it, and, believe me, everybody else knows it. The less decisive you are in dealing with it, the more problems you'll have later with the other employees. Cut out the cancer early and quick.

If you have clients, as I do, you'll want to get tough and quick about ridding yourself of nuisance clients, too. Skip Ross, a very successful distributor in a direct sales organization, impressed on me that vacuums fill. Skip said: nature abhors a vacuum. Nature will do just about anything to fill a vacuum. If you'd like some nice, new clothes, go through your closet and take all the stuff you don't wear to a charity. Leave two-thirds of that closet starkly empty. You'll be amazed at how fast that thing will fill back up. This "principle of vacuum" has served me very well over the years. Just about every time I say no to or fire a troublesome, high-maintenance client, that vacuum quickly fills with better business. I know you'll find this to be true, too.

Do Not Look a Gift Horse in the Mouth. Get On, Hang On, and Enjoy the Gallop.

Our duty as men is to proceed as if limits to our ability did not exist.

—Pierre Teilhard De Chardin, French clergyman

What plans would you have on your drawing board if you knew you could not fail?

—Reverend Robert Schuller

There are those times, those days, those "spurts," when you can do no wrong.

Every football fan knows about The Drive, John Elway's remarkable last-minute scoring drive in 1986 that robbed Cleveland of a trip to the Super Bowl. And we saw Elway do it more than once. We saw Staubach and Stabler do it. We saw Joe

Montana do it. Even journeymen quarterbacks like Dave Krieg have done it. We watched more contemporary quarterbacks pull one of these off. We've seen entire teams play poorly for three quarters, then suddenly seem to emerge from lethargy and ineptitude to score more points in four minutes than in the previous 40. And, if you're with a group of people watching one of these fantastic finishes, some will always, logically ask, "Hey, why didn't he play like that during the game? Where was all this talent an hour ago?"

These guys suddenly get into "a place" where there's magic. They can do no wrong. They can't fail.

Earl Nightingale once observed "that a time can come for each of us when more will happen to us in six months than transpired in the previous five years. Compound events in our lives can be compressed into remarkably short periods." This is a phenomenon. It is often the payoff an entrepreneur gets from years of hard work, struggle, and sacrifice. It is peak productivity time. Everything works. Opportunities abound. Doors swing open easily. Recognition, even celebrity, occurs. Income soars.

When The Phenomenon occurs, everything speeds up. If you're accustomed to a few new client prospects developing in a week, you'll be flooded with a big multiple of that. The worthwhile demands on your time multiply like rabbits. Here's what you do. Say "Thank You." Sleep less, gulp more vitamins, and go with the flow. Be alert for this happening, then fan the fire. For a brief time, you will want to loosen up your cautions about taking on more than you can handle and embrace it all.

When The Phenomenon occurs, it's doubly important to be on guard against anybody or anything that may snuff out the fire. Do not let yourself be distracted by any time- and energy-sucking, jealous, needy, incompetent, lazy, vampirous malcontent. Squash 'em like a bug.

Some people just can't stand prosperity. Their own emotional and psychological inner mess causes them to start setting up roadblocks to slow things down if good things start happening too quickly. If this is a business partner, friend, or—gulp—spouse, guess what you've got to do? I have an acquaintance I'll not name who is married to one of these people who just cannot stomach success. She's a great mate, right up until his career shifts into high gear. Then she gets physically ill with mysterious diseases. She starts picking fights. She wrecks the car. I've watched him slammed to a stop by this roadblock-builder several times. Watch out for such a person in your life.

Now, back to The Phenomenon itself. I cannot tell you how to turn it on. But I can tell you about a few of the factors and conditions that seem to be present when it occurs. First, it seems to happen to already hyper-productive people. Second, it comes to people already in hot pursuit of worthwhile, well-defined goals. Third, it seems to occur to people who have "stepped up" in associating with other high-performance people. Fourth, it often starts out with a single "big break"—which you've got to be astute enough to recognize and massively exploit.

You can create the conditions in your life most likely to spark The Phenomenon. Then embrace it!

CHAPTER 12

The Inner Game of Peak Personal Productivity

My mother said to me, "If you become a soldier you'll be a general;
if you become a monk, you'll end up as the Pope." Instead,
I became a painter and wound up as Picasso.

—PABLO PICASSO

ou can load yourself up with big, hunky day planner devices, computer software, notepads, different colored pens, stickers, strings tied around your thumbs, and a million little "techniques," and you'll still be pitifully unproductive if you don't have your "inner game" under control. Productivity is an inside-out game.

Psycho-Cybernetics and Getting More Value from Your Time

You probably recognize the term "Psycho-Cybernetics." The book of that title has sold more than 30 million copies worldwide, and several different audiocassette adaptations have been sold via the famous Nightingale-Conant catalog, the Sybervision catalog, and a television program, and published and distributed through bookstores by Audio Renaissance. The mental training techniques created by Dr. Maxwell Maltz that make up Psycho-Cybernetics have been endorsed and used by famous pro athletes and coaches, leading corporate executives, star salespeople, entertainment personalities, and by me. Salvador Dali gave Dr. Maltz an original painting as thanks for Psycho-Cybernetics' influence on his career.

When Dr. Maltz first began putting his techniques down on paper in the 1960s, he was far ahead of his time, so far ahead that people first discovering his material right now are amazed by and profit enormously from them.

What does all that have to do with you and peak productivity?

There is a certain state of mind that best facilitates achieving peak productivity. You can best create that state of mind as needed, when needed, at will, by mastering certain Psycho-Cybernetics techniques.

For example, Dr. Maltz talked about "clearing the calculator." If you have a simple calculator laying around, get it, and take a look at it. You'll find that you have to hit the "clear" button and either store in memory or completely clear away one problem before you employ the calculator to solve another. In his studies of human behavior, Dr. Maltz observed that all too often we're trying to use our minds to work on several problems at once, without ever stopping to hit the "clear" button.

Achieving maximum personal productivity requires that you become extraordinarily facile at stopping, storing, and clearing, so as to direct 100% of your mental powers to one matter at a time, to the matter at hand. One client of mine, the CEO of a $20 million-a-year corporation, is a compulsive, obsessive worrier. He admittedly lets a dozen worries loose to run around in his mind at the same time, while he is trying to do something else and says he is constantly interrupted by his own thoughts. He marvels at me and tells others that "it is amazing how Kennedy can just box up a problem, put it away on a shelf in his mind, focus totally on some task, and only go back to work on the problem when he wants to." This is because I have practiced and practiced and practiced the technique of "clearing the calculator" until it is second nature to me.

A big reason for my prolific output as a writer is that I never have to "get in the mood' to write. Many people go through great physical and mental gyrations just getting ready to get ready to write. I don't. I can sit down, put my fingers on the keys, clear my calculator in 60 seconds or less, and write.

This is just one of a number of simple but very powerful Psycho-Cybernetic techniques, but it illustrates a very important point: *if you can't control your thoughts and manage your mind, you can't control or manage your time.*

It's for this reason that I urge you to get free information from www.psycho-cybernetics.com.

Creating a Peak Productivity Environment

You can do a number of things to make certain that your environment works *for* you instead of against you. The following are some key ideas to consider and experiment with.

- Psychological triggers
- Organization vs. clutter
- Feng shui

As I said, I am a big believer in populating my work environment with "psychological triggers"—objects that remind me to think a certain way. I work at mentally attracting wealth, for example, so my primary work environment is full of things that represent wealth; at last count, 27 such pictures, objects, and artifacts were within view. Because I am very concerned with time, I have eight clocks around me. I have a wooden hangman's noose to remind me of deadlines. A painting on my wall of a black tiger devouring a man in the jungle reminds me of the quote "Tigers starve last in the jungle," and reminds me to be tough and aggressive.

A good friend of mine who is very successful at his endeavors has a little plaque on his car dashboard that says: "People Are Good, Business Is Great, Life Is Terrific!" He wants to see it every time he makes or takes a call on his car phone or gets out of the car to go on an appointment.

I think you can "surround yourself" three possible ways:

1. By accident and happenstance, with no purpose in mind and no purpose served
2. Consciously or unconsciously, with things that trigger negative responses, frustration, anger, resentment, depression
3. Deliberately with things selected to reinforce positive—productive—responses.

"A Clean Desk Is a Sign of a Sick Mind"

Let's not be dogmatic about this. I suspect that a person with a constantly, pristinely clean and neat desk and work environment—a "Felix"—may very well be neurotic. Certainly I *prefer* to believe that. On the other hand, the person immersed in clutter and a chaotic environment—an "Oscar"—MUST waste time by hunting and searching, must be distracted. There is a broad band of acceptable style between the two extremes.

Personally, fortunately, largely by "clearing the calculator," I can sit down and work effectively surrounded by clutter or in chaos. However, I will tell you that I am most productive in what I have come to call a "semi-organized environment." As a writer, for example, I think it's unavoidable to have stacks of papers, reference materials, and other documents around, but I find it very helpful to have those piles organized by topic or project.

Really creative, innovative thinking seems to come out of chaos more often than out of neatnik organization. But the successful implementation of innovative ideas seems to come about in a most organized, disciplined way.

It's worth noting, to paraphrase management guru Peter Drucker, that what we are after is *effectiveness*, not necessarily *efficiency*. Put a time-and-motion analyst on the typical entrepreneur and he will come up empty; how do you analyze the guy who sits on the floor of his office watching daytime TV talk shows and thumbing through magazines for hours on end, then suddenly hits upon the right "pitch" for his company's new fitness product?

The most important thing here is to be honest with yourself. Is the level of clutter and disorganization around you helping or hindering? Out of control or just about right?

> One big time-saving tip I can give you is:
> when in doubt, throw it out.

Many people are compulsive keepers. I find a bit of ruthlessness toward paper is beneficial. If you seriously doubt you will need or use it again, go ahead and throw it out immediately. If it becomes really important, it will be provided to you again. At least once a year, usually in December, I conduct a violent purge of my correspondence files, client records, desk drawers, etc., and throw out as much of it as I dare. In all these years, I've had that come back to haunt me only a couple of times.

N ot too long ago, I moved much of my home office, files, records, and library from one home to another. More than 100 boxes. Because I'm busy, some of those boxes have yet to be opened, two years later, and that's because no need has sent me into them, looking for anything. Undoubtedly, by the time I get around to opening them, I'll be able to throw out what's in them. Which probably means it didn't need to be kept in the first place. I'm making a note to myself: be even MORE ruthless.

It's also important for your "workspace" to make it easy for you to work. My own, in my home office, is not unlike a pilot's cockpit; without getting out of my swivel chair, I can operate my computers, my word processor, my TV and VCR, my audiocassette recorder, and my calculator. I can reach my most important reference books, and I have two "surfaces" for paperwork. Once you get to work, you ought to be able to stay at work without having to jump up and down every minute or two to fetch something or put something else away.

The cordless phone is a marvelous invention. If you talk on the phone a lot, as I do, this enables you to roam, stretch, relax in a recliner, go find a file, even go outdoors while talking.

Now What the Heck Is Feng Shui?

Never let it be said that I don't bring my readers the new and different. *Feng shui* is the latest Eastern philosophy to be grabbed by businesses and individuals in the West. Literally translated, it means "wind and water," and more broadly translated, it is the art of improving your productivity, creativity, and good fortune by making the relationships between objects in your environment and yourself more harmonious. You might think of it as acupuncture for the office—blocked energy can be made to move more freely.

Just for example, rearranging furniture or replacing a solid wall with a see-through fish tank might create good feng shui. William Spear, the author of a book on this subject, *Feng Shui Made Easy: Designing Your Life with the Ancient Art of Placement*, likes to tell of being called in to consult with the owners of a failing hotel, the Kings Cross Hyatt in Sydney. By relocating an escalator in the main lobby, money was "attracted" instead of "repelled," and the hotel zoomed to a high occupancy rate with no other changes made.

Feng shui experts believe that you can create a "wealth corner" in a room and that you can create a "feeling" in a room conducive to exceptionally productive work. They also believe, as in the case of hotels and restaurants, that feng shui can make a property more inviting and comfortable to visitors and guests.

Maybe you find all this a bit "woo-woo-ey." But some very serious business leaders don't. In Hong Kong, big, blue-chip companies such as Jardines and The Hong Kong Bank spend a fortune on feng shui. Architects routinely consult with feng shui experts. And it's reported that gambling casino designers use feng shui to create "bad luck areas" for the customers.

Short of hiring your own feng shui consultant, how can all this help you? Well, when I first read about it, I was struck by its conceptual compatibility with my long-held belief that environment matters and matters differently to different people. This means that, just like you have a time of day when you are at your best (and a time of day when you are at your worst), you probably have an "environment" that helps you be your best, too. You may feel different when surrounded by one color scheme vs. another, one style of furniture vs. another, in a room with or without a big window, with living things like plants or birds in the room, and so on. I don't think most people give this much thought at all but probably should.

If you feel like getting very specific with feng shui, here's one application: assume that the door to your office is always at 7 o'clock. Look at 11 o'clock; that area represents wealth; 12 o'clock represents fame; 1 o'clock represents relationships. Let's say there's an old, maybe chipped or broken bookend holding up a dusty pile of books and magazines in "wealth." Cleaning that up, dusting off the books, keeping only some magazines, getting a new bookend, could release "wealth energy" and improve your fortunes.

Here, I think, is the bottom-line: the space we work in, the way that space is organized, the tools we use, the objects and colors we see, the noises we hear, the smells we smell all combine to have an impact on our productivity, and on our ability to be productive. Much of this is common sense. Some is just slowing down long enough to think about yourself and your reactions to different stimuli. If you want to get in deeper with disciplines like feng shui, you can. Why not give yourself the advantage of a high productivity, success environment?

Finally—the Militant Attitude

I have come to really, deeply, vehemently, violently *resent* having my time wasted. I place a very, very high value on my time, and I believe that the value you really, honestly place on your time will control the way others value it and you.

I have talked about this elsewhere in this book and do not want to redundantly beat up on any one single point, yet this self-determination is so important. You set your own price. And you determine whether or not people "get it" and respect it.

When I was in direct sales, managing, motivating, and trying to help others build their businesses, I was constantly amazed and often depressed at how little value people placed on their time and how pitifully unwilling they were to protect it and wisely invest it. I heard "I didn't because . . . my mother-in-law decided to surprise us with a visit . . . my buddy Bob dropped by and took up the whole evening . . . the roof started to leak and I had to work on that . . . ." Etc. Etc. But if you already had something very important to do, that you were committed to doing, mother-in-law would have to sit home alone and watch TV, buddy Bob would be bounced out, a bucket would be put under the leak, and you'd stay focused.

How tough are you on those who would undervalue your time? How tough are you on yourself?

CHAPTER 13

Reasons Why a Year Passes
and No Meaningful
Progress Is Made

The only thing some people do is grow older.

—EDGAR HOWE, AMERICAN JOURNALIST

I wonder how many times I've heard a variation of "I've got 30 years' experience—I *should* be doing better"; or "I work very hard—I *should* be doing better"; or "I've got my Ph.D.—I *should* be doing better"; or "I've got the best product—I *should* be doing better." Etc.

In the speaking business, I know many people believe they are much better speakers than I am. Some of them are right, and they are befuddled and antagonized by how well I've done, mystified at how I came to be on the giant public events with huge audiences and they didn't. "I'm better" or "I've been at this longer"—"*I should be up there instead of him.*"

I suppose the biggest problem with all that is the word "should." It implies "entitlement." And our entire nation is being rotted out by the viral spread of "entitlement thinking."

Everybody seems to think they are somehow entitled to something. The Indians think they are entitled to become tax-exempt multimillionaires through gambling because of wrongs done to their ancestors. Minorities believe they are entitled to college admission and jobs based on quotas, regardless of their qualifications. Women believe they are entitled to all sorts of special treatment from employers so they can have children, raise a family, and develop a career; "have their cake and eat it too." Senior citizens believe they are entitled to government benefits far in excess of whatever they paid in, to free medical care for life, regardless of how long they live or who has to pay. We even have a nutcase congressman who has suggested that every American is entitled to a home and a job, and that our government should guarantee them these things. The so-called "Gen Xers" seem to think they are entitled to everything, right now, for doing nothing. And I could keep going. (Have I offended everybody yet?)

> Here's the real deal: nobody's entitled to anything but opportunity. Not even to a level playing field. Nothing. Nada. Just opportunity.

This is one reason why a person fails to advance much from one year to the next; he is so busy whining about how unfair everything is and feeling sorry for himself that he has no time left to make anything happen.

But, as Eric Hoffer, author of *The True Believer: Thoughts on the Nature of Mass Movements*, wrote: *"There are many who find a good alibi far more attractive than an achievement*, for an achievement does not settle anything permanently. We still have to prove that we are as good today as we were yesterday. But when we have a valid alibi for not achieving anything, we are fixed, so to speak, for life. Moreover, when we have an alibi for not writing a book and not painting a picture and so on, we have an alibi for not writing the greatest book and not painting the greatest picture. Small wonder that the effort expended and the punishment endured in obtaining a good alibi often exceed the effort and grief requisite for the attainment of a most marked achievement."

Hoffer's observation is one of the finest, most accurate, and profound I have ever encountered.

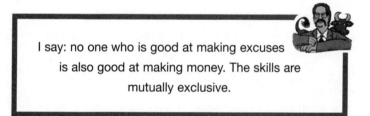

I say: no one who is good at making excuses is also good at making money. The skills are mutually exclusive.

Alibi-itis. "I'd do that IF . . . ." The kids were grown. I wasn't so tired after a day's work. I had more support from my spouse. I had a better education. I didn't live in this terrible neighborhood. And on and on and on.

How about writing a book? Scott Turow, now one of the wealthiest and most successful fiction authors of our time, wrote his first novel longhand, a page at a time, while riding the train, commuting to and from the offices of his law practice. My friends Mark Victor Hansen and Jack Canfield wrote and had published or self-published God knows how many books, audiocassettes, and entire courses with the world barely noticing. They received rejection notes from ALL the major publishers for their "ultimate brainchild" before convincing a small publisher to put out *Chicken Soup for the Soul*, which has since become a juggernaut, an empire, with hundreds of titles and millions of copies sold. How about breaking into acting? Sylvester Stallone kept his belongings in a bus station locker, slept in alleys, and scrounged food from dumpsters early in his career.

So, reason number one: alibi-itis. Choosing a nifty alibi over a difficult path to achievement. That's why somebody looks around after another year has passed and is still in exactly the same place.

Majoring in Minor Matters

It never ceases to amaze me how people can manage to focus their time, energy, and resources on everything but the few vital things in their business that really have to do with directly making money.

Just recently, a fellow heard me speak at a seminar, rushed to the back of the room and bought my "Magnetic Marketing System," came back to me and enthusiastically told me how much he learned from my talk and how excited he was about implementing my ideas, pumped my hand like Jack LaLanne, and tore out of there like the Tasmanian devil. About a week later, his copy of my System came into my office with the mailman, with a note sheepishly asking for a refund. On arriving home, the man discovered he already had my System, sitting on a shelf, still shrink-wrapped in plastic, purchased at a seminar over a year earlier. Now, it's not the fact that it was my System, but what on earth had he been doing every hour of every day for a year that was more important than enhancing his business' ability to attract and acquire new customers?

Not long ago, I did a bit of consulting for a guy with a small chain of retail stores. He just about begged for my help. Said he wasn't making it and had no money to do any advertising or marketing with. I gave him a simple, easy-to-implement idea—a change in the way incoming calls were handled—that would easily double his sales. I know it would. It's proven. After a few months passed, I asked him how that strategy was working. He explained that he'd been too busy to try it. *Too busy doing what?* He couldn't tell me. Just too busy.

Well, here's how to get focused, if you're having trouble in that department: identify and write down the three most important, most significant, most productive, most valuable things you can do to foster success in your particular enterprise. Just three. Write them down. From there, translate them into three actions you can take each and everyday. Write them down.

For example, one of the most important things to me is a continuous stream of new requests for my services. As long as this demand for "me" exceeds the available supply of "me," I can demand and get premium fees, insist on first-class travel, choose clients I like and blow off those I don't, choose projects that interest me and reject those I don't, confidently turn away business knowing the temporary vacuum will fill, and generally do as I darned well please. But if I let the demand diminish so that supply exceeds demand, I have to start compromising all over the place. So this is very important to me. What can I do every day to be certain this demand-supply ratio stays weighted in my favor?

I do not let a day go by that I do not send out a letter or a package, make or return a phone call, get an article published, do something to keep my books on bookstore shelves, secure a high-profile speaking engagement, or do something else to create and stimulate "deal flow." It doesn't matter how busy I am. Or how tired I am. Or if it's the Friday before a holiday weekend. Whatever. Before sunset, at least ONE thing will be done intended to stimulate demand.

Nothing and no one can steal the time required to make certain that happens. Every single day. No exceptions. No excuses.

As a direct result, "demand" for me has steadily grown, even as the "supply" I am willing to offer has diminished, which has allowed me to very substantially raise my fees, keep raising them every year, fire troublesome clients without remorse, and do business entirely on my terms, to suit me. This one single, simple discipline has been worth millions.

But I'll bet if you followed the typical entrepreneur around with a list of his "Big Three," you'd log lots of days where he "never got around to" doing any one of those three things at all. See, those days are failure days. Too many of those days guarantee you'll wind up on New Year's Day just about where you were 365 days before.

Breaking the Code of Extraordinarily Successful People

Early in my career, I was very fortunate to be exposed to some of the greatest "success educators," such as Earl Nightingale, Dr. Maxwell Maltz, Napoleon Hill, and, the more contemporary Zig

Ziglar and Jim Rohn. More recently, for ten years, I got to appear frequently as a speaker on programs with Rohn, Zig, Brian Tracy, Tom Hopkins, and others like them.

Jim Rohn is a very interesting fellow. You've undoubtedly seen Tony Robbins on television. Did you know that Jim Rohn was one of Tony's earliest coaches, mentors, and employers? If you want real, well-grounded "meat" from someone in the personal development area, it's hard to beat Jim Rohn. Anyway, there's a point Jim makes that stuck with me when I first heard him say it, when I was a kid, and that still has impact when I hear him talk about it today. It breaks the code of the highly successful person. It takes all the mystery and mystique away. When you very closely examine the highly successful person, in any field, you walk away saying to yourself:

Well, it's no wonder he's doing so well. Look at everything *he does.*

You see, success isn't much of a mystery. In that respect, it's actually disappointing to a lot of people who want it to be very complicated, who, as we discussed earlier, prefer a good alibi. But it's just a reflection of what you are doing with your time.

I would now add to Rohn's statement, ". . . and look very closely at the one thing or two or three things he gets done without fail, every single day."

I can do a good job of predicting what your bank balance will be a year from now, if you'll give me the following information:

- What's in the account today
- A list of the books you read and tapes you listened to last month
- Some information about the five people you hang out with most

---

CHAPTER 13 / REASONS WHY A YEAR PASSES AND NO MEANINGFUL PROGRESS IS MADE

- A little analysis of how you spend your time during an average week

For 90% of all people, by the way, making this prediction is a no-brainer. The correct guess is: same as it was last year.

If you happen to be "stuck," then just taking *some* action to change isn't even enough. Jim Rohn calls this *"The principle of massive action."* And when you look at highly successful people, you'll find they are massive action takers. They don't just try one solution to a problem, they implement 20 all at the same time.

I once had a dentist call me, after having gone home from my weekend seminar, and tell me: "I've made a list of 300 things to change in the practice." Every week, he did ten of them. After 30 weeks, he had done everything on that list, big and small. And, without a penny increase in advertising, without a dollar's difference in marketing, in the same office, with (almost) the same staff, his practice had more than quadrupled in volume. He took massive action. When I tell the story, the usual, predictable reaction is astonishment and dismay—*"Three hundred* changes? I'd never get 300 things done."

I've had the interesting experience of spending just a little bit of time personally with Lee Iacocca, and I have studied him a lot from afar. Iacocca did not rescue Chrysler by doing one thing. Or one thing at a time. He took massive action. He pursued the government-backed bailout, he slashed operating costs, he rushed the design and release of exciting new cars, he went on TV personally in Chrysler's commercials and took his case to the public, he boldly put forth the strongest warranty in the history of the auto industry, he negotiated with the unions and the employees. And it's no wonder he saved that company. Look at everything he did.

CHAPTER 14

Commonly Asked Questions
and Answers About Peak
Personal Productivity

Although it has been some years since I've conducted time management seminars, the questions my clients, subscribers, and friends asked these days about being more productive are not very different from questions asked by workshop participants years ago. In this chapter, I answer the most frequently asked questions. Hopefully, these include the questions you've been wanting to ask.

Q: I just read a book titled *Don't Set Goals*, yet you insist that successful entrepreneurs all set goals. I've never been good at it myself. Is it really necessary?

A: The subject of "goals" or "goal-setting" is a very big umbrella.
    What most people mean by goal-setting is writing down, usu-
    ally in some detail, lists or collections of long-term, medium-
    term, and short-term goals. Most time management systems
    include weekly and daily to-do lists, which are really
    another way of listing goals. And most goal-setting teaching
    breaks down goals by category: business or career, financial,
    personal, social, family, love relationship, self-improvement,
    spiritual, and so forth. And *I would say that there are a lot more
    successful entrepreneurs who follow this approach than there are
    who don't.*

    Also, for many people, the disciplined act of focusing on
    questions such as *What do I really want? What do I want my
    business to be like in three years?* and writing down answers is
    very productive in and of itself. *I've never known or met a suc-
    cessful entrepreneur who wasn't a list maker.* So I think it's diffi-
    cult to mount a good argument against goal-setting. As you
    get really good at goal-setting, get more in control of your
    mind, and get more successful, you may do less of it and may
    be a bit sketchier or broader in your view, but you'll still benefit
    from the process. Personally, I have a bank of short-, medium-
    , and long-term goals, some very clear and well-defined,
    some fuzzy and evolving. I tend to work on them and check
    my actions against them at least once a month.

    As I understand it some lecturers contend that most people
    just won't set goals, so why teach what people won't do? Not
    much of a case, I think when you understand that highly suc-
    cessful people do what most folks aren't willing to do in all
    aspects of behavior. Actually, the fact that 90% or 95% of the

people randomly surveyed have never written down detailed goals and have no intention of doing so is the best argument of all for doing it. When I did a lot of speaking on this topic (I now specialize in seminars on marketing), I used to spring this on audiences: I'd pull out a big wad of $100 bills and offer one to each person with some kind of written goals on them in pockets, purses, or briefcases. Typically, with 100 salespeople or entrepreneurs in a room, I'd only have to give away a few bills. But here's what's instructive: when I would later quiz those people, I'd routinely discover that the ones who got the $100 bills needed them least because they were the most successful individuals there.

Q: **What do you do when you fail to hit a goal? Or, more mundanely, find that you can't meet a deadline?**

A: Let's take the second one first. Business is all about the setting and meeting of deadlines. Meeting them is usually a combination of being adept at estimating or forecasting the amount of time you'll need, then blocking out that time, as we discussed in this book, delegating or obtaining help if possible, and having the self-discipline to do what proves necessary to get the job done.

If you are going to miss a deadline, and you wonder what to do, just do the right thing. Doing the right thing is magic. I've spoken a number of times at events where General Norman Schwarzkopf has also been a speaker. His topic, appropriately, is leadership—although every point he covers applies equally well to peak personal productivity, because we are our own leaders. Anyway, one of his keys is simply "Do the Right Thing." And, you know, we almost always know what the right thing to do is. We may not like it. We may not want to do it. But we know what it is. And when we do it, we gain stature in the eyes of others, we gain self-esteem, and we gain personal power.

As to a missed goal, I think "failure" is too harsh of a word, in most cases. If every coach, coaching staff, and team who set out to win the Super Bowl quit trying the first time they missed getting there, we'd watch the same two teams in the Super Bowl year after year, forever. Actually, a high achiever's secret that was taught to me very early in my career defies logic, but it works. Here it is: don't reset the same goal. Don't back off to a less ambitious goal. Instead, create a similar but bigger and more exciting goal with a new, appropriate time line.

Failure is a part of success. The most commonly used illustration is Babe Ruth, "The Home Run King," famous for his 714 home runs. But he also struck out 1,330 times. R.H. Macy failed in seven businesses before hitting a home run with the now-famous Macy's Department Store. The batteries we use in our cars, in flashlights, in toys, and in electronics all exist as a result of Thomas Edison striking out with five years of experiments. You have to learn to master failure in order to have success.

Q: **When you delegate, when you turn things over to other people, aren't you inevitably going to have a lot of problems, foul-ups, even outright theft?**

A: Different businesses have different kinds of problems in this area. But there are two overriding supervisory rules that you'll want to remember. One: *expect the best.* Expectations have enormous impact on results. And conveyed expectations have great impact on most people. Most folks are smarter and more capable than we give them credit for. Some never get challenged. But rule number two is: *know that you only have the right to expect what you inspect*. If you want to know what happens with zero accountability and zero supervision, read the novel *Lord of the Flies*. The fact that performance improves with measurement and accountability to someone else has been proven everywhere from sports to weight loss to business. So, you have to walk a fine line between empowering and encouraging but not turning loose; between inspecting and critiquing but not micro-managing.

Q: **What's the biggest single problem with delegating? And what do you do about it?**

A: The biggest problem is with the little things. Let's say you ask someone a question; says he has to check records or otherwise get the answer for you, but he never does that unless you remember to ask him again. What do you do about it? Suffer. Make notes and remember to ask again. Of course, you can insist that your employees jot these things down. Or you can do everything by memo; you create a paper blizzard, but you have total accountability. For me, this area is the most frustrating part of dealing with employees or associates.

Here is the best insurance policy against things falling through the cracks: for each person you delegate to, have a list of everything, big or small, that you turn over to that person. As each one responds, you can mark off the items. Every so often, check the list for the lagging items. Frankly, this is a bit cumbersome. However, I've used it off and on over the years, and it's the only reliable control method I've found.

When I was office-bound for a few years, I used a storyboard. One whole wall in my office was cork-covered, and in one section there was a vertical section for each person I worked with. I always had a little stack of 1½ x 2½-inch square cards with me. Whenever I gave someone a question, task, project, whatever, I wrote it on a card, dated the card, and stuck it up on the wall. When they came back to me with the completed task, I took the card off. In an instant, at a glance, I—or anybody else—could see who was working on what. And this worked pretty darned well.

Q: **What about the idea of only doing things you really like to do? Some people teach that as a success strategy.**

A: Well, I've never advocated that. I just saw an article in our local newspaper with a photo of a homeless man sitting under a tree reading a book, and the caption said that this man passed his time doing only what he wanted to do: reading great literature and playing cards with friends. But he's *homeless. I think doing only what you want to do is a prescription for poverty.* But diverting as much of your time as you can to those few things you do extraordinarily well, that's a prescription for peak productivity. You can never eliminate doing some things you dislike and some things you may not even do well. I like speaking, especially to large audiences, and I like being highly paid for doing so. I hate travel, but I found out they won't bring those really big audiences to my house. So I got good at traveling. I still don't like it, but I'm a savvy, efficient, comfort-and-convenience trick-laden road warrior. I don't particularly like pitching my books and tapes from the platform either; I'd rather just speak, get a standing ovation, and get back in the limo. But if I want to appear at certain events, and if I want to make $20,000.00 to $50,000.00 or more per speech, I've got to sell my stuff—and do a damned good job of it. So I've gotten quite good at it. So good that other speakers pay me sizable fees to help them do it better.

I've read a few really airy-fairy, way-way out there meta-physical authors who insist they'd rather do only what they enjoy, without exception, and be poor than do things they don't like doing in order to have material things. Some of these guys are outright phonies: telling large numbers of lazy people what they want to hear in order to separate them from what little money they have. Others really believe what they are saying but are, privately, insanely jealous of others who do well. I know one such sackcloth-and-ashes lecturer and author who, although pretty well known, barely scrapes together a living each year, who insists that he is happy and that happiness counts more than material wealth. But mention Tony Robbins to him and he goes on a 20-minute tirade. He is violently jealous of Tony's phenomenal financial success and his fame. And that reveals what he really wants. I've concluded that, one way or another, these folks are full of B.S.

Highly successful people do what they *need* to do, whether they like it or not, in order to get the results they want. This is objective orientation versus activity orientation. BUT don't miss the point that you should redirect energies to the few things you do best at every opportunity.

Q: **How do you conquer procrastination?**

A: Heck if I know. I procrastinate. And I believe everybody does. Fortunately, the things I do it with most are relatively trivial. For example, I hate shopping, so anything I can't buy out of a catalog, I usually don't buy until it's a blatant, urgent necessity. Most of the successful entrepreneurs I know tend to be most productive under deadline pressure and often need imposed or self-imposed pressure to get into a difficult task. The often taught advice is: first, do what you want to do least. Sometimes that works for me, sometimes it doesn't. I also think there are areas where you SHOULD procrastinate. For example, if I have an idea, question, decision, or whatever, and I can't make a decision quickly, I'll deliberately set it side for a period of time before revisiting it. I have a procrastination place" for reading material that can wait and a "procrastination pile" for correspondence or other work that has no particular urgency. I'm always amazed at how much of that stuff takes care of itself when it is left alone for a few weeks or months.

I think the important thing is to be honest with yourself. If you are putting something off, don't pretend otherwise. And it's also important to keep controlling, setting, and addressing your own priorities rather than reacting to those of other people. Too many overloaded entrepreneurs still operate on the "squeaky wheel gets the grease" basis. Although that is understandable and although it can provide survival, that philosophy cannot produce peak productivity. You want to be the one making very deliberate decisions about how you invest your time—then stick to those decisions as much as possible.

Lisa Kanarek, author of the fine book *Organizing Your Home Office for Success,* uses the term "selective neglect." See, "selective" means you are in control, doing the selecting and doing it for the right reasons.

Q: **I'm a salesperson, and I wonder: how can I sell effectively to super-busy people like you? Entrepreneurs and CEOs who do not have a minute to spare.**

A: The way to get through to us is the same way you get through to anybody; it's just that the need to hit it right on the mark is magnified with us. *The key is speaking to our self-interest.* If you can perfectly match your message, your promise to MY fears that haunt me at night, MY concerns that are foremost in my mind right now, and MY desires that I would kill to fulfill, then, believe me, you'll get as much of my time as you want. Most salespeople are much too product- and process-oriented, not sufficiently prospect-oriented.

You have to come to grips, totally, with the unhappy fact that these busy prospects do not have one whit of interest in your product, your company, your company's credibility, your prices—none of that. You've just got to let loose of all those concepts. You must put together what I call a "Magnetic Marketing Message" that focuses on things of prime, over-riding interest to the people you want to reach.

For example, a few years ago I did a little pro bono consulting with the Arizona Chapter of the Arthritis Foundation about securing more, new corporate sponsors for their telethon. The Foundation couldn't get the key CEOs it wanted to talk with to give them the time of day. That's because

Foundation representatives were talking about the Arthritis Foundation. I created a new message aimed at these CEOs—telling them about new, creative, very-low cost opportunities to get massive, prestigious public recognition for their companies featuring prime TV advertising at about 25 cents on the dollar vs. what they would normally pay. I created a letter that played to their egos, presented a logical case, had something new to offer, and hit the fear button—that their competitors might beat them out for an exclusive. Some of these busy CEOs called the very same day they got my letter. Companies such as Federal Express and Domino's Pizza raced to get involved.

If you're going to sell to me, for example, there are six, maybe seven, things of such enormous interest to me that would force me to drop whatever I was doing, suspend my skepticism, and give you my undivided, enthusiastic attention. If you can figure out what one, or some, of those things are and link yourself and what you offer to those interests, you break through. If you don't, odds are excellent that the busyness of my schedule will shut you out.

Q: **How do you handle all of your communication? You must get a zillion letters, faxes, and phone calls.**

A: You're not kidding. I get a lot of correspondence. I try to make instant decisions and move the paper immediately and quickly whenever I can. With people I work with frequently, I'll often type my response right on the bottom or even up the side of the letter or fax they sent me. I also try to throw out everything I can. Even though I need to read my "junk mail," as a practitioner of direct mail, I keep only a few pieces for my files. I save only the documents I need, and throw out the envelopes and enclosures. If I can't act on something immediately, my next preference is to get it into my Tickler Files. If I can pick up the phone and deal with something quickly and easily, I do it. Oh, and my incoming mail is screened, so a few things get handled without me even seeing them. And I'm able to delegate some stuff immediately. The big goal is to avoid having piles of paper that you haven't acted on, haven't filed, don't know where to file, but aren't willing to throw out.

As an aside, when asked what one, single quality he looked for in his top associates, Lee Iacocca said "Decisiveness." I look around today in business—and government—and I'm dismayed at the inability and unwillingness of the so-called leaders to make a decision, clearly enunciate it, and stand up for it. The more decisions you make and the faster you make them, the more productive you are.

Q: What's the worst mistake you can make related to productivity?

A: Losing control. To anything or anybody. Control and productivity are inextricably intertwined. How can you be productive if you are not in control? It follows, then, that the more control you exert, the more productive you are.

The minute you get diverted to dealing with somebody else's priorities at the expense of your own, you're headed down a very slippery slope. Doesn't matter if that happens because somebody is hovering in your doorway, sending a fax, calling, whatever. You can't let it happen. When I had a fairly large staff, I had people hang in my doorway for 20 minutes while I refused to visually or verbally acknowledge them before they finally gave up and left. My own habit, when I'm in town, is often to do a little bit of reading, easy paperwork, and organizing in the evening while watching television. I prefer to regroup in the evening for the next day. But if I don't, the first thing I do the next morning—after my writing time—is to regroup, reorganize, and establish my priorities for the day. As each day goes along, people spring things on you, unexpected good things as well as unexpected bad things happen, and the firm grip you have on your time is forcibly loosened. At the end of the day, you've got to put things back together so you can begin the next day with a firm grip.

Resource
Directory

This directory will give you information to contact the people and access the resources listed throughout this book. In this directory, you will find many of the people listed chapter by chapter, based on the first reference to them in the book.

Chapter 1

Yampolsky, Mace. Contact: 702-385-9777/fax 702-385-3001.

Martin, Dr. Charles. Contact: 804-320-6800/fax 804-320-1014.

Furey, Matt. Author, *Combat Conditioning*, and popular author, coach, and seminar leader in health, fitness, martial arts, anti-ageing. As an entrepreneur, Matt has achieved extraordinary success marketing a variety of information products via the Internet and conducts "boot camps" teaching Internet marketing, publishing, and entrepreneurship. Contact: www.matt furey.com. Note: Matt is also the master-licensee and publisher of the Psycho-Cybernetics Foundation courses. www.psycho-cybernetics.com.

Milteer, Lee. Author, *Success Is an Inside Job*, speaker, entrepreneurial coach. Lee is a much-sought-after speaker on prosperity, embracing change, and success strategies, with clients including Federal Express, the Disney companies, and NASA. Contact: www.leemilteer.com.

Chapter 2

Petito, Dave. Contact: 760-773-9022.

Chapter 3

Rowland, Chet. Chet provides thousands of pest control business owners with advertising and marketing systems, Web sites, customer newsletters, training, seminars, and field trips to his pest control company and "Chetland" in Tampa, Florida. Contact: 888-444-0442/fax 813-932-5642.

Chapter 5

Nightingale, Earl. One of the earliest "voices" of modern self-improvement and success education, author of the *Lead the Field* audio program, and co-founder of Nightingale-Conant Corporation. Today, Nightingale-Conant publishes audio programs by hundreds of leading authors, speakers, and experts ranging from Dan Kennedy to Brian Tracy to Lee Iacocca. Contact: 847-647-0300/fax 847-647-9243.

Chapter 6

Vance, Mike. Former close confidante and associate of Walt Disney's, directly involved in original planning for Epcot, Mike is the most entertaining, fascinating speaker and storyteller in the area of entrepreneurial creativity and author of *Think Outside the Box*. Contact: 440-243-5576/fax 440-243-8754.

Rohn, Jim. Contact: 800-929-0434.

Chapter 7
LeGrand, Ron. Former "grease monkey" turned outrageously successful real estate investor, Ron now teaches his "Quick Turn-Fast Cash" real estate techniques to thousands of independent investors each year. Contact: 904-262-0491/fax 904-262-1464; Web site: www.GlobalPublishingInc.com.

Hill, Napoleon. Recommended books: *Think and Grow Rich* and *Succeed and Grow Rich through Persuasion.*

Chapter 9
Maltz, Dr. Maxwell/Psycho-Cybernetics. The late Dr. Maltz was the father of "self-image psychology," and his original book *Psycho-Cybernetics* has sold more than 30 million copies worldwide. Dan Kennedy and several associates acquired rights to all Dr. Maltz's works, and in recent years Kennedy has co-authored *The New Psycho-Cybernetics*, *The New Psycho-Cybernetics* audio program by Nightingale-Conant, and *Zero Resistance Selling.* Psycho-Cybernetics is, in essence, a scientific approach with practical mental training techniques to improve all aspects of personal performance. Info @ www.psycho-cybernetics.com.

Chapter 10
Fatt, Rory. President, Restaurant Marketing Systems, Inc. Rory provides thousands of restaurant owners with advertising and marketing systems, Web sites, customer newsletters, training, and an annual conference. Contact: 604-940-6900/fax 604-940-6902.

Chapter 11
Paul, Jeff. Author, *How To Make $4,000.00 a Day Sitting at Home in Your Underwear,* a book about his mail-order/direct marketing

experiences, which has sold more than 200,000 copies. Contact: 630-778-0018/fax 630-778-0019.

Chapter 13

Hoffer, Eric. Author, *The True Believer.*

Hansen, Mark Victor/Canfield, Jack. Authors, *Chicken Soup for the Soul* books. Contact: 949-764-2640; Web site: markvic torhansen.com.

Ziglar, Zig. One of America's most popular, celebrated motivational speakers for three generations. Zig's book, *See You at the Top* is a true classic. Contact: www.zigziglar.com.

Tracy, Brian. Brian Tracy is one of America's most sought after and popular professional speakers, author of dozens of business books, including *Turbo-Strategy: 21 Ways to Transform Your Business;* and a visionary thinker about business trends, opportunities, and strategies. Contact: www.briantracy.com.

Hopkins, Tom. Tom Hopkins is world renowned as a master sales trainer. *Sell It Today, Sell It Now,* on compact disc and co-authored by Pat Leiby, is an excellent resource for learning how to lower sales resistance and increase sales acceptance in potential clients. For more information contact him at info@tomhopkins.com. Receive free sales content, tips, and closes by subscribing to Tom's selling skills e-newsletter at www.tomhopkins.com.

Chapter 14

Kanarek, Lisa. Author, *Organizing Your Home Office for Success,* and other books about organization skills.

Other Books by the Author

No B.S. Business Success, Entrepreneur Press

No B.S. Sales Success, Entrepreneur Press

Ultimate Sales Letter, Adams Media

Ultimate Marketing Plan, Adams Media

Make Millions with Your Ideas, Penguin

The New Psycho-Cybernetics, Prentice-Hall

Zero Resistance Selling, Prentice-Hall

Author's Web Sites

www.dankennedy.com

www.dankennedyproducts.com

www.renegademillionaire.com

www.psycho-cybernetics.com

To Contact the Author Directly

Phone: 602-997-7707

Fax: 602-269-3113

Time Truths

Dan Kennedy's #1 No B.S. Time Truth

If you don't know what your time is worth, you can't expect the world to know it either.

• • • • •

Dan Kennedy's #2 No B.S. Time Truth

Time Vampires will suck as much blood out of you as you permit. If you're drained dry at day's end, it's your fault.

• • • • •

Dan Kennedy's #3 No B.S. Time Truth

If they can't find you, they can't interrupt you.

• • • • •

Dan Kennedy's #4 No B.S. Time Truth

Punctuality provides personal power.

• • • • •

Dan Kennedy's #5 No B.S. Time Truth

By all means, judge. But know that you too will be judged.

• • • • •

Dan Kennedy's #6 No B.S. Time Truth
Self-discipline is MAGNETIC.

• • • • •

Dan Kennedy's #7 No B.S. Time Truth
If you don't MANAGE information, you can't profit from information.

• • • • •

Dan Kennedy's #8 No B.S. Time Truth
Good enough is good enough.

• • • • •

Dan Kennedy's #9 No B.S. Time Truth
Liberation is the ultimate entrepreneurial achievement.

Preface to

No B.S. Business Success

Just a spoonful of sugar helps the medicine go down.

—R. SHERMAN, FROM *MARY POPPINS*

W elcome to what I sincerely hope is the most truthful, blunt, straightforward, non-sugarcoated, no pabulum, no holds barred, no-nonsense, no B.S. book you have ever read on succeeding as an entrepreneur.

I wrote the first edition of this book back in 1993, and since then, I've personally heard from thousands of readers from all over the world. You saw a few of their comments on the opening pages of this book. It struck a chord with entrepreneurs; the chord of authenticity. No college classroom theory, no baloney. Real world truths from somebody who succeeds day in, day out, as an entrepreneur, working without a net. Since then, a lot has happened in my life, business and personal. For example, I've sold two businesses I built up; walked away from a very important and lucrative nine-year business relationship; made well-planned, continual, evolutionary changes in my other businesses; gone through a divorce after 22 years of marriage; been diagnosed diabetic; and more. I'm pleased to report I'm happier than I've been in many years and am living the life I set out to live.

Anyway, all these changes, new experiences, and lessons I've learned from my clients certainly warranted a complete updating of this book.

It is a personal book, me talking straight with you, as if I was consulting with you and as if we were sitting around at the end of the day on my deck, watching the sunset, enjoying adult beverages, and just hanging out. Because it is personal, along the way I'll be telling you quite a bit about me and about my business life—past, present, and future. None of this is about bragging. I have no need for that or interest in doing it. What I share, I tell you so that you understand the basis for the advice and opinions I dispense.

I have occasionally been introduced as The Professor of Harsh Reality. This does NOT mean I'm negative. If anything, I'm one of the most optimistic, positive-minded people you'll ever meet. However, I do not believe in confusing positive thinking with fantasy. And the word *optimism*, like many words in our perplexing English language, has more than one meaning. There's a mammoth difference between earned, deserved, justified optimism and wild-eyed, blue-sky, stubborn optimism.

I've discovered that I'm most successful when I have a firm grip on what is and least successful when caught wrestling with what ought to be.

In this book, I've tried to share, from my 25-plus years of entrepreneurial adventure, what *is*. Not what *should be* or what is only in theoretical books, classrooms, or seminar rooms.

If You Are Already in Business for Yourself

This book will help you go forward more astutely, efficiently, productively, and confidently. I think you'll also catch yourself nodding as you go along, saying to yourself, "This guy has been where I live." Sometimes there is value in just finding out you're not alone! The very first "success education" that I was ever exposed to was a set of recordings by Earl Nightingale titled *Lead the Field*, that I listened to when I was in my early teens. In those tapes, Nightingale gave me badly needed permission to violate the norms I saw around me, with his dramatic statement:

> *If you have no successful example to follow in whatever endeavor you choose, you may simply look at what everyone else around you is doing and do the opposite, because—THE MAJORITY IS ALWAYS WRONG.*

That may not be a precise, verbatim quote; but it is what I recall and have stored in my subconscious as a primary guiding principle. This leads to my strategy of deliberately questioning all industry norms, deliberately violating most of them, and encouraging my clients to do the same. It also led to my coining of the term "Mediocre Majority" to succinctly describe the vast undistinguished middle of any industry or profession. Anyway, Earl said a lot of things I had been thinking but had never heard anyone validate, and that gave me a great boost of confidence and conviction. Maybe some of my words, here, will do the same for you.

Most entrepreneurs tell me that the feeling they get from this book make them instantly eager to share it with other entrepreneurs. Please do so! If you want some place to send them, refer to www.nobsbooks.com.

If You Have Not Yet Started in Business but Intend To

This book might scare you off. If it does, consider it a favor; you're too easily spooked to succeed anyway. The entrepreneurial arena is no place for the timid, nervous, or easily worried to come and play.

If it doesn't scare you off, it will help you avoid many pitfalls and problems and help you cope with those that can't be avoided. It will not cover the basics. There are plenty of books out there on the basics, and we're not going to cover the same ground all over again. This is not a how-to-start-a-small-business book. This is a go-for-the-jugular success book.

As I said earlier, I am not a fuzzy-headed academic, pocket-protector-and-wingtip-shoes accountant, or other theorist, although plenty of these pretenders write business books. I'm also not a retired authority who runs a business in my memory. I've been on the firing line meeting a payroll, battling the bankers and bureaucrats, struggling to satisfy customers, and solving real business problems. Over years, I've arrived at a point where my own business is engineered to meet all my lifestyle preferences—for example, only one employee, in a distant office, not under-foot; no set hours; no unscheduled phone calls. But still, I deal with clients and vendors and real business life just like you do. I also work very hands-on with clients in a wide variety of busi-nesses, as well as being "the consultant to the consultants"—I advise more than 50 different leading marketing and business consultants, each exclusively serving a different business or pro-fessional niche, in direct, hands-on relationships with more than one million small business owners. I want you to know this because I think it makes this book more valuable to you.

I'll never forget taking over a company with 43 employees, never having managed more than two people in my life. I grabbed every management book I could get my paws on and sucked up all the experts' advice. Then, after a couple of months of getting my brains beat in every day by my employees, I started to look critically at the credentials of those "expert" authors. Most of them had never—I repeat, never—managed a workforce. These geniuses spewing out creative management, nonmanipulative management, Japanese management, open-door management, and everything-else management wouldn't have survived a week in the real world. I resent those authors to this day. And it's a shame that a lot of college kids get that management theory, that is, fantasy sold to them as reality. So, I chucked all their books, rolled up my sleeves, used my common sense, and started finding out what really works and what doesn't.

Ever since then, I look at every new business book with suspicion. Most won't pass muster because most can't pass the real-experience test. I was originally motivated to write this book largely because reading most of the other books written for and sold to entrepreneurs turned my stomach.

I also want you to know that there are a lot more things I haven't got a clue about than there are things I understand; in this book, I have not dealt with any of the many things I'm in the dark about. Everything in here is based on my own expensive experience. It may not be right. You may not agree with it. But at least you should know that I didn't swipe it out of somebody else's book, give it a jazzy new psychobabble name, and pass it off as a new miracle tonic.

It's about Getting Rich

I also know you can't eat philosophy. So, although there is a lot of my own philosophy in this book, its primary job is to show you how to make more money then you ever imagined possible, faster than you can believe possible. This is a book about getting rich. If that offends you, please put this book back on the shelf or take it back to the store and get a refund. Spend your money on milk and cookies instead. You'll be happier. In fact, I'd like to quickly clear up a big misconception about what being an entrepreneur and owning and building a business is all about. The purpose is *not* to employ people, *not* to do social good, *not* to pay taxes. A lot of liberals think those are the purposes of business. Nuts to them. The purpose of being an entrepreneur is to get really, really rich, and reward yourself for taking on all the risk and responsibility with exactly the kind of life and lifestyle you want. Facilitating that is the sole aim of this book.

Before getting into the "meat," on the next few pages, you'll find a brief description of my business activities past and present and my current business in the back of the book beginning on page 247. I think you'll benefit more from the book if you understand where I'm coming from; however, you can choose to skip these pages if you like and jump right to Chapter 1. Your choice.

I'd like to explain the *Mary Poppins* quote at the top of this Preface. *Mary Poppins* was one of the first movies I was taken to see in a theater as a child. I watched it just the other night on cable TV and enjoyed it thoroughly. If you've seen it, you can probably call up the scene of Julie Andrews and the children singing the "just a spoonful of sugar helps the medicine go down" song. It's a lovely thought. (Or as she would say, "loverly.") In real business life, however, the emotional need for spoonfuls of sugar is very dangerous. How well you can take medicine— deal with reality—has a great deal to do with how successful you are as an entrepreneur.

There's a legendary book by Napoleon Hill I hope you've read, titled *Think and Grow Rich*. In that book, he enumerates 17 success principles adhered to in common by the hundreds of history's greatest entrepreneurial achievers he studied, interviewed and worked with, such as Andrew Carnegie, Henry Ford, Thomas Edison, and so on. Of the 17 principles, the one everybody seems to like the least and ignore the most is "accurate thinking." I believe it to be the most important one. So this book, my book, is heavy on that principle. It is medicine without the accompaniment of sugar.

Finally, let me say that, when I graduated high school, my parents were flat broke. I started with no family money. I didn't step into a family business. No one handed me anything on a silver platter. At age 49, I am semi-retiring, a multimillionaire, free to live precisely as I choose, indulging my interest in horse racing. It was all made possible through the kind of thinking, attitudes, habits, and strategies I've laid out in this book. I have been blunt, forthright, and held nothing back.

With that said, I still hope you not only profit from this book, but enjoy reading it. And I welcome your comments, thoughts, or questions. You can communicate with me directly by fax, 602-269-3113.

—Dan S. Kennedy

Preface to
No B.S. Sales Success

There are basically four types of salespeople: sales professionals with strong ambition who are eager to strengthen and fine-tune their skills; sales professionals who are jaded, close-minded, cynical, and stuck; nonsalespeople who realize they need to be, such as doctors, auto repair shop owners, carpet cleaners; and nonsalespeople who either do not recognize they need to be or are resistant to the idea.

Ambitious Salespeople 1	2 Stuck Salespeople
3 Nonsalespeople Eager to Learn	4 Resistant Nonsalespeople

This book will resonate with those in the first and third quadrant. It will be wasted on the others. I've spent more than one-fourth of an entire lifetime, more than 25 years, working with people in both the first and third quadrant—and doing my level best to avoid the folks in the second and fourth. This book literally summarizes the most important strategies I've developed over those 25 years—some originating from my own experience, others originating from my observation of super-successful sales pros' behaviors that I have converted to replicatable strategy.

There are a great many things this book is NOT. It is NOT, for example, a textbook approach to selling. It is not about moral or spiritual philosophy (those matters are left to you). It is only slightly about the psychology of selling. It is noticeably free of trendy new terminology, buzzwords, and psycho-babble so many sales trainers and authors seem to be fond of. And it is not a motivational book either. If you need someone else to motivate you, you have far bigger problems than this book might tackle. Or any hundred books, for that matter.

This is simply a straightforward, relentlessly pragmatic, "no b.s." *presentation of what REALLY works in selling.* Not what should work. Not the academic theories about selling. What REALLY works.

You may not thoroughly enjoy this book. It may make you uncomfortable. Confronting, challenging, and rethinking long-held beliefs and habits is provocative and often profitable but rarely comfortable or enjoyable.

My aim is very simple: after reading this book, I intend for you to implement behavioral and procedural changes that will immediately and dramatically increase the income you earn from selling. This book is all about putting more money in your pocket, nothing loftier than that, nothing less than that. And if we have to break a few eggs to make that omelet, then that's what we'll do.

You might want to know that this book has had a long former life. It was first published in 1994, has been in print continuously through 1996, a 2nd edition was published in 1999, which was in print through 2001, and now this thoroughly updated and substantially expanded in this new edition. Why is it important for you to know you've wound up with "the sales book that will not die" in your hands? Two reasons. First, as evidence you've gotten your paws on strategies that ARE really valuable and that DO really work. Successful salespeople recommend this book to each other, they stream to the bookstores and demand it. Even when a publisher has lost interest in it, the marketplace has insisted this book be put back onto the store shelves. (By the way, now you can tell others about this book by sending them to www.nobsbooks. com, to get free excerpts.) Second, you will see references in the book that are obviously dated, or references to my writing of its first edition, and I didn't want you to be confused by that; thus, this explanation.

Now, to the important stuff: quick, practical actions you can take to make selling easier, less stressful, more fun, and much, much more lucrative and rewarding.

About the Structure of This Book

This book is divided into six parts. In Part 1, I describe the 15 strategies I use most in selling. Each is a stand-alone application, and any one of them alone could significantly improve your results in selling. But they can also be linked together differently for different situations for increased value and power.

In Part 2, I deal with what goes on before selling can even begin: finding, attracting, and getting into a selling situation with a prospect. As you'll see, I'm no fan of the way most salespeople carry out this job. Here you'll discover some rather radical ideas.

In Part 3, I provide a framework for selling. The various pieces described in Parts 1 and 2 can be plugged in and out of this structure.

In Part 4, I share with you the dumbest things salespeople do to sabotage themselves.

In Part 5, I reveal my personal, best, most valued, contrary approach to selling. It may not be for everybody; it may not be for you. Frankly, I argued with myself about putting it in or leaving it out. I ultimately decided I would not be playing fair with you if I sold you a book about selling and held back the information most responsible for my own success. Use it as you will, and good luck.

In the last decade, the sales world has been flooded with new technology, and Part 6 of this edition contains an updated section on my "no b.s." observations of this.

—Dan S. Kennedy

Index

Special Free Gift #1 from the Author

Free Kit of Kennedy Peak
Personal Productivity Tools

A collection of self-analysis tests, checklists, and forms to manage and measure your personal productivity, ten "psychological trigger" cards to post in your work areas, and the "Stake through the Heart of the Time Vampires" illustrated 8½ x 11-inch mini-poster, all FREE, as thanks for buying and reading this book.

Also, FREE REPORT: "The Misunderstood Link Between Kennedy-Style 'Magnetic Marketing' And Time: Five Biggest Marketing Mistakes That Waste Time and Destroy Productivity."

TO OBTAIN YOUR FREE PRODUCTIVITY TOOL KIT AND FREE REPORT: There is no need to damage your book by tearing out this coupon—a photocopy is satisfactory. Complete ALL the information required, then either fax this form to 410-727-0978 or mail to Glazer-Kennedy Inner Circle, 200 W. Baltimore St., Baltimore, MD 21201. Allow 2 to 3 weeks for delivery. Providing information below constitutes permission for Glazer-Kennedy Inner Circle to contact you with information about its products and services.

Name _____

Business name _____

Address _____ ❏ Business ❏ Home

City/state/zip or postal code _____

Phone _____ Fax _____

E-mail address _____

Special Free Gift #2 from the Author
Copy this Page and Fax this Form to: 410-727-0978

FREE

Test Drive Three-Months of Dan Kennedy's
"Elite" Gold Inner Circle Membership
Receive a steady stream of marketing and business building advice

Yes Dan, I want to take you up on your offer of a FREE Three-Month Gold Inner Circle Membership, which includes:

1. Three months of your *No B.S. Marketing Newsletter*
2. Three months of your Exclusive Audiocassette Interviews
3. Three months of your Marketing Gold Hotsheet
4. Special FREE Gold Member Call-In Times
5. Gold Member Restricted Access Web Site
6. Continually updated Million Dollar Resource Directory
7. Open fax line
8. At least a 30% discount to future Glazer-Kennedy events and seminars

There is a one time charge of $5.95 to cover postage for ALL three months of the FREE Gold Membership and you have no obligation to continue at the *lowest* Gold Member price of $39.97 per month ($49.97 outside North America). In fact, should you continue with membership, you can cancel at any time by calling Glazer-Kennedy Inner Circle at 410-951-0147 or faxing a cancellation note to 410-727-0978.

Name _____ Business name _____

Address _____ ❏ Business ❏ Home

City/state/zip_____ E-mail _____

Phone _____ Fax _____

Credit card ❏ Visa ❏ MasterCard ❏ American Express

Credit card number _____ Exp date _____

Signature_____ Date _____

Providing this information constitutes your permission for Glazer-Kennedy Inner Circle LLC to contact you regarding related information via mail, e-mail, fax, and phone.